Tony & Giorgio

Tony & Giorgio

Tony Allan and Giorgio Locatelli

Photographs by Jason Lowe

Grafton

This edition specially produced for The Wonderful Book Company in 2003

First published in Great Britain in 2003 by
Fourth Estate
A Division of HarperCollinsPublishers
77–85 Fulham Palace Road,
London W6 8JB
www.4thestate.com

10 9 8 7 6 5 4 3 2 1

A catalogue record for this book is available from the British Library
ISBN 0-00-766402-8

Design and Art Direction by Caz Hildebrand
Project coordination by Terry Durack

Printed in Great Britain by Butler & Tanner

For my *nonno*, Mario Caletti, and my *nonna,* Vicenzina Tamborini, who slaved over the stove as I grew up, and taught me respect and honesty. **Giorgio**

For my father, who talked me out of going into the building trade; for my mum, who talked me into becoming a chef; and for Denys and the kids who gave me a reason to get up at 2.30 in the morning for fourteen years. **Tony**

Contents

Italy v. England

I remember very well the first time I ever tasted Marmite.
It was also the last time I ever tasted Marmite.
Giorgio

giorgio

To an Italian, life is an opera, a drama. Every little thing that happens is like front-page news. If someone drops a glass on the table, it's a major incident. Everyone yells, everyone has an opinion, it's chaos.

Italians have a totally different lifestyle from the English. The sun has a lot to do with it, of course. We spend a lot of our life outdoors, and it makes us more outgoing, more expressive. Maybe that's why we yell and gesticulate so much. Basically, deep down, we're all drama queens.

The Italian writer Umberto Eco once said that we Italians are who we are because, throughout history, we were the ones who could sit down and do nothing. It sounds strange but the fact is we have raised the act of doing absolutely nothing to a fine art. We call it *non far nulla*, and it is something that every Italian understands instinctively. The English don't have these instincts and feel somehow guilty if they do nothing. They always have to be doing something, and that's why they're always on the move.

In England, if you do nothing you're a loser. In Italy, the people who do nothing are running the country. What does that tell you?

tony

We Brits are hard working, methodical and unemotional – and that's the good side of our character. We're stoic, proud and strong, and we place great importance on politeness and 'doing things properly'. If Italians are opera performers, then the English are the opera critics, sitting back, considering, analysing and judging.

It's not that we don't have emotions, because we do. It's just that we believe that showing them in public simply isn't good form. The worst thing an Englishman can do is embarrass himself. So it's easier not to take the risk and not to stick your neck out – not be the loudest, the tallest or the silliest.

As a nation, we'd much rather stew about something than get it off our chest. If you ask diners in your restaurant if they've enjoyed their meal, they'll say, 'Yes, of course!' And then they'll go home and write the most vicious letter to you, outlining everything that went wrong with it.

Italians are different. They act first and think later. When I was in Rome, I bought a slice of pizza from a little pizza joint. It only cost a quid but after I took my first bite the owner ripped it out of my hands and gave me another slice. 'I could tell from your expression that you weren't enjoying it,' he said. 'This one is better.' That's not really an English thing to do.

To Italians, food is the most important thing in their lives (the second most important thing is how they look). This obsession is based on their belief that eating good food isn't a privilege, it's a basic right.

Everyone eats well in Italy. Eating well is a sign of well being, of the normal functioning of a family. It doesn't matter whether they're eating in an expensive restaurant or buying a *panino* (bread roll) from a kiosk at a railway station, they will still insist on the best. And if they don't get it, they will complain – loudly, of course.

In truth, there is really no such thing as Italian food, because the individual regions of Italy are so strong and distinct. Sicilian food is nothing like the food of Tuscany, while Sardinian cooking is a million miles from the cuisine of Emilia Romagna. There are still a lot of people in Italy who will only eat the food of their own particular region. When I was growing up, chilli was something you would never find in our kitchen, because chilli was from the South and I came from Lombardy, in the north. I don't think my grandfather ever tasted a chilli in his whole life. I can't take my father to a restaurant because he won't eat anything that isn't from the north. It's a real pain, but I respect him for it.

Wherever you grow up in Italy, however, you grow up with food. I often think about the times as a little boy when I would walk in the mountains with my grandfather. We would drop into Cecchino the baker's and buy his freshly baked *michetta* rolls. Then we would go to the *salumeria* and buy a hunk of *mortadella di fegato* (liver sausage). Then we would sit down on a big stone wall and my grandfather would pull out his hunting knife and slice up the sausage. A bite of sausage, a bite of bread – the flavours were fantastic. Whenever I think about that wall, I can still taste that mortadella. I once took my kids there and showed them the wall, but I don't think they were terribly impressed. To them, it was just a wall.

The big day of the week was always Tuesday, when my grandparents would close their restaurant and my grandmother would cook a big lunch for all the family and friends, usually about sixteen of us. It was such an event. If my grandmother wanted to cook rabbit, for instance, my grandfather would bring her the rabbits, she would pick out the one she wanted, and he would kill it, skin it and prepare it for cooking, right there in front of us. It wasn't anything horrible, just a natural thing to do.

These days, children don't have that sense of death being a part of life. I once brought home a live crab and cooked it with spaghetti for dinner. When the kids sat down at the table and looked at the crab in the pasta, they both turned and stared at me. 'You're an assassin!' they yelled.

I can't imagine what would happen if I brought home a rabbit.

giorgio

I am naturally drawn to Italian things. I drive a Ferrari (that's when my mate, Vinnie Jones, hasn't commandeered it), I wear Italian clothes and I love Italian furniture. If I go more than a few days without pasta, I start getting withdrawal symptoms. Giorgio, of course, rides about on English-built motorbikes and puts on English manners but says things like '*pero*' and '*allora*' and '*andiamo*' all the time. I'm a would-be Italian but I talk like a Cockney geezer.

For me, it's the simple things Italians do best: like an honest plate of spaghetti, a good loaf of crusty country bread just pulled out of a wood-fired oven, or a magnificent new-season white truffle from Alba shaved over a freshly made risotto. That's real food, and real flavour.

But it's not just the flavours, it's the way they're put together. I am knocked out by the theatrical way in which the Italians stage-manage everything they do.

I've always felt envious of Italians. What you can never take away from them – whether you're talking Italian footballers or Italian chefs – is their unfailing sense of style. Let's face it, *they look better than us*. Even if they lose a game ten–nil, the Italian football squad still look better, move better and hold themselves better than the winners.

Being Italian, Giorgio has been born with a passion for food already in his veins. Being English, I had to find this passion for myself. It's the difference between a highly trained chef and a self-taught cook. My passion is self-taught.

tony

on English food

My mum was a very good but very English cook. The most exotic thing she ever made was pavlova. There was no such thing as Caesar salad or rocket salad or Tuscan bread salad for her. In our house, salad was usually some tomato and lettuce and not much more. I guess that explains this inbred craving I have for salad cream.

I was brought up on comfort food, like shepherd's pie, eggs and bacon, and steak and kidney pudding. I also inherited my father's love of Scotch eggs, pork pies, and pickles such as gherkins and pickled onions. I remember when I was five or six, I picked up a pickled onion from my dad's plate and popped it into my mouth. That sharp, tongue-curling hit of vinegar was such a shock, yet such a pleasure.

Ironically, we never had fish in our house. My father was allergic to seafood, which didn't help. So my first real experience of fish was at the school canteen, when they served up glowing yellow, artificially dyed smoked haddock in tinned tomato sauce. I remember standing there feeling like Oliver Twist in reverse: 'Please sir, I don't want any more.' It was horrible of course and, to add insult to injury, I got a bone stuck in my throat. It's a wonder I ever became so passionate about fish.

The turning point was discovering fish and chips. What a great dish. Suddenly the world seemed a sensible place once again.

When I was growing up, meals were just fuel stops. It was stop, fill up the tank, and you're off, without having to think too much about what you've just put in your gob. Things have changed enormously in Britain since then.

There is some pretty remarkable food in this country. For my money, British produce is the best in the world but we rarely do it justice. English apples are sensational. Our oysters, our venison, our wild fish and our cheeses are all bloody brilliant.

Show me a perfectly cooked standing rib of beef with fresh horseradish sauce and roasted English onions, a new season's grouse straight from the oven, a wheel of carefully aged farmhouse Cheddar, and some magnificent wild Scottish salmon poached in a simple court-bouillon, and I'll show you why we haven't got a thing to be ashamed of.

I love English food – chicken tikka masala, hummous and spaghetti bolognese. You can't get more English than that.

When I worked at the Savoy, I started to appreciate English food. I soon discovered steak and kidney pudding, which taught me how good food in this country could be. The kidneys and steak would be cooked slowly and then left overnight to build up flavour and character. Then they were put in a big bowl and covered in a mixture of flour and fat from the kidney, and the whole thing would be steamed for about two hours. When it was finished, you could push your fork in through the pudding and the steam would rush up into your face while the aroma wrapped itself around you. For something that wasn't Italian, it was amazing.

I also love Yorkshire puddings, and the great British Sunday roast, and those marvellous bread and butter puddings. But not all English flavours are so thrilling. I remember very well the first time I ever tasted Marmite. It was also the last time I ever tasted Marmite. And I can't stand English–Italian food – chicken surprise and spaghetti bolognese. It's terrible.

It took me four years to discover the one true *pièce de résistance* of English cooking. When I was at the Savoy, I was taken to Smithfield meat market early one morning and experienced my first full English breakfast. It was all there: the salty, thick-cut bacon, the just-runny egg, the kidneys, the fruity black pudding, the greasy sausage, the baked beans, the thin, buttered toast. I loved it. Suddenly I started to understand the English.

giorgio

Recipes
Italy v. England

Parsnip and smoked haddock soup

Tortellini in brodo

Prawn and langoustine cocktail

Insalata di fagiolini con cipolle rosse arrostite

Salad of cauliflower, ham hock and Stilton

Carpaccio di manzo

Steak and kidney pudding

Insalata di spinaci e ricotta salata

Slow-roasted belly pork with apple sauce and baked
cabbage

Pappardelle ai fegatini di pollo, salvia e tartufo nero

Salt beef with carrots and mustard dumplings

Coniglio al forno con prosciutto crudo e polenta

Spezzatino di pollo al limone con carciofi

Rhubarb bread and butter pudding

Tiramisu

Real sherry trifle

Parsnip and smoked haddock soup

Zuppa di pastinaca con eglefino affumicato

Good smoked haddock is an art form, and it's something that really only exists in the UK. In this soup it plays off the sweet nuttiness of the parsnips beautifully, producing a flavour combination that is unmistakably British. **Tony**

Serves 6

25g/1oz butter
1 onion, finely chopped
1 celery stalk, finely chopped
1kg/2¹/₄lb parsnips, finely chopped
1.8 litres/3 pints vegetable stock
300g/10oz undyed smoked haddock

300ml/¹/₂ pint milk mixed with
   300ml/¹/₂ pint water
150ml/¹/₄ pint double cream
   (optional)
sea salt and freshly ground black
   pepper

Heat the butter in a large saucepan, add the onion and celery and cook for about 5 minutes, until softened. Stir in the parsnips and cook for a further 5 minutes. Pour over the stock and bring to the boil. Simmer gently for 20–25 minutes, until the parsnips are very tender.

Meanwhile, place the smoked haddock in a frying pan and pour over the milk and water. Bring to the boil and simmer for 2 minutes, then remove from the heat and leave the fish to cool in the poaching liquid.

Blitz the parsnip mixture until smooth, either with a hand-held blender or in a jug blender. Add the cream if required, then reheat gently and season to taste. Remove any skin and bones from the smoked haddock, discard the poaching liquid, and flake the fish into the soup. Ladle into warmed bowls to serve.

Tortellini in brodo

Tortellini in broth

What a great dish this is. Add just two or three tortellini and you have a lovely, light soup. Put a lot more in and you have a terrific pasta dish sauced with a soupy broth. I love this served with a big wedge of Parmigiano to grate on top.

'OO' flour is a special Italian fine flour used for making pizza and pasta. It is available at larger supermarkets and in Italian food shops. **Giorgio**

Serves 4

1.5 litres/2¹/₂ pints chicken stock
   (see page 241)

For the pasta:
250g/9oz Italian 'OO' flour
large pinch of salt
1 egg, plus a little beaten egg for
   brushing
3 egg yolks
1 tablespoon olive oil

For the filling:
200g/7oz skinless, boneless chicken
   breast, diced
25g/1oz pancetta, chopped
25g/1oz mortadella, chopped
1 tablespoon double cream

To make the pasta, sift the flour and salt into a food processor, then slowly pour in the egg and egg yolks through the feed tube, followed by the olive oil. As soon as the mixture comes together into a dough, switch off the machine. Put the dough on to a lightly floured work surface and knead for 10–15 minutes, until smooth, then wrap in clingfilm and chill for about 30 minutes.

Meanwhile, make the tortellini filling. Put all the ingredients in a food processor and whiz to a paste. Transfer to a bowl and chill until ready to use.

Cut the pasta dough in half and flatten it slightly with a rolling pin. Pass each piece through a pasta machine on the widest setting, then fold in half and repeat, each time switching the pasta machine to a finer setting, until the pasta is about 0.5mm thick. With a 6cm/2¹/₂in pastry cutter, cut a circle from the pasta and, using your fingers, stretch it as thinly as possible. Brush the edges with a little beaten egg and place a little of the filling in the middle. Fold the pasta over the filling to make a semi-circle, press the edges together to seal, then fold the 2 corners up over the centre and squeeze together tightly. Repeat until all the pasta and filling have been used. Keep the pasta dough covered with a damp cloth while you are working, to stop it drying out.

Bring the chicken stock to the boil and drop in the tortellini. Simmer for about 4 minutes, until the tortellini are tender, then ladle into bowls and serve.

Prawn and langoustine cocktail

Cocktail di scampie e gamberoni, salsa
'Marie Rose'

A survivor from the good old days when dining out meant prawn cocktail followed by sirloin steak followed by Black Forest gâteau. Yes, it did get a bit naff for a while, but treat it with respect, add a couple of fresh langoustines, and this classy first course will knock everybody's socks off. If you want to add more langoustines, then go right ahead. **Tony**

Serves 4

1 cucumber, peeled
1/2 iceberg lettuce, shredded
300g/10oz peeled cooked prawns
8 large cooked langoustines,
    shelled
pinch of paprika
1 lemon, quartered

For the cocktail sauce:
6 tablespoons Tony's mayonnaise
    (see page 244)
2 tablespoons tomato ketchup
3–4 shakes of Tabasco sauce
1 tablespoon cognac
squeeze of lemon juice

Make the cocktail sauce by mixing together the mayonnaise, ketchup, Tabasco, cognac and lemon juice.

Run a vegetable peeler down the length of the cucumber to make long, thin ribbons. Place in a large bowl with the shredded lettuce and toss with a tablespoon of the cocktail sauce. Divide the lettuce and cucumber between 4 serving bowls and pile the prawns loosely on top. Arrange the langoustines on top and spoon the remaining cocktail sauce over the prawns and langoustines, allowing it to trickle down. Dust sparingly with paprika and then serve immediately, with the lemon wedges and a few slices of buttered brown bread.

Insalata di fagiolini con cipolle rosse arrostite

Bean salad with roasted red onions

I always think green beans aren't shown off to the best of their ability in this country. Usually they're just boiled up in water and served with a knob of butter on top. It's a pity, when you realise they have so much more to give. **Giorgio**

Serves 4

2 shallots, finely chopped
50ml/2fl oz red wine vinegar
3 red onions
125ml/4fl oz olive oil
750ml/1¹⁄₄ pints red wine
100ml/3¹⁄₂fl oz white wine vinegar
2 tablespoons caster sugar

250g/9oz extra-fine green or yellow beans
2 tablespoons freshly grated Parmesan cheese, plus Parmesan shavings to garnish
sea salt and freshly ground black pepper

Put the shallots in a small, non-metallic bowl and pour the red wine vinegar over them. Cover and leave to marinate overnight.

Preheat the oven to 200°C/400°F/Gas Mark 6. Wash the red onions, but don't peel them, then rub them with a tablespoon of the olive oil. Place them in a roasting tin, cover tightly with foil and bake for about 1 hour, until tender. Leave until cool enough to handle, then remove the skins, trying not to squash the onions too much.

Put the wine in a saucepan and boil until it has reduced to a few tablespoons and become shiny and syrupy. Remove from the heat and stir in the white wine vinegar and sugar. Slice the roasted onions, place them in a deep bowl and cover with the reduced wine mixture.

Cook the green beans in boiling salted water for about 5 minutes, until just tender, then drain and refresh under cold running water. Add the remaining olive oil to the marinated shallots. Toss the shallot mixture with the green beans and grated Parmesan and season to taste.

To serve, arrange the red onions on 4 serving plates and top with the green beans and shavings of Parmesan.

Salad of cauliflower, ham hock and Stilton

Insalata di cavolfiore, garretto di maiale e Stilton

This is what I call the best of British – new-season cauliflower, a nice, meaty pig's knuckle and a dressing made with one of Britain's greatest cheeses. This is not your normal, everyday salad but an exciting combination of top-rate produce. If the dressing is too thick, use a little of the ham stock to thin it down. **Tony**

Serves 6

2.5kg/5½lb ham hocks
1 onion, halved
2 celery stalks, roughly chopped
chopped parsley

For the Stilton dressing:
2 egg yolks
4 tablespoons white wine vinegar
1 teaspoon Dijon mustard
300ml/½ pint olive oil

50g/2oz Stilton cheese, crumbled
salt and white pepper

For the cauliflower:
4 peppercorns
1 sprig of rosemary
1 bay leaf
1 tablespoon olive oil
1 large cauliflower, cut into florets

Place the ham hocks in a large saucepan with the onion and celery and cover with cold water. Bring to the boil and simmer gently for 4–5 hours, topping up the water level if necessary during cooking to keep the ham hocks covered. The meat should be almost falling off the bone. Leave to cool in the liquid, then flake the flesh from the ham hocks with your fingers and set aside.

For the Stilton dressing, make sure all the ingredients are at room temperature. In a bowl, beat the egg yolks with a little salt and white pepper, half the vinegar and the mustard. Add the oil a drop at a time, whisking constantly to give a thick, glossy mayonnaise; you can start to add the oil in a thin stream once about a third of it has been incorporated. In a separate bowl, beat the remaining vinegar with the Stilton, whisking well until smooth. Then stir this into the mayonnaise. Taste and adjust the seasoning.

For the cauliflower, put the peppercorns, rosemary, bay leaf and olive oil in a large saucepan with 1 litre/1¾ pints water. Bring to the boil and then drop in the cauliflower florets. Cook for about 5 minutes, until tender, then drain and refresh under cold running water.

Place the cauliflower in a serving bowl and arrange the flaked ham on top. Drizzle with the Stilton dressing, add parsley and serve.

Carpaccio di manzo
Beef carpaccio

Beef carpaccio was invented by Giuseppe Cipriani in Venice's Harry's Bar in 1961, and named after an Italian artist known for his use of vivid red colours. The Harry's Bar original is dressed with a mixture of mayonnaise, Worcestershire sauce and lemon juice, but here are four variations that work just as well. Because there is nowhere to hide, only top-quality beef will do for this dish. **Giorgio**

Serves 4

550g/1¼lb beef fillet
sea salt and freshly ground black
**   pepper**

For the broccoli topping:
1 small head of broccoli
juice of 1 lemon
3 tablespoons olive oil

For the caper and mayonnaise topping:
2 tablespoons Tony's mayonnaise
**   (see page 244)**

2 tablespoons capers, rinsed and
**   drained**

For the mayonnaise topping:
2 tablespoons Tony's mayonnaise
**   (see page 244)**

For the rocket topping:
2 handfuls of rocket
1 tablespoon olive oil
1 tablespoon lemon juice
75g/3oz Parmesan shavings

Trim the fat from the beef fillet, then cut it into thin slices. Place 3 or 4 slices on a sheet of clingfilm or baking parchment, cover with another sheet of clingfilm or baking parchment and bash with a meat mallet or rolling pin until the meat is paper thin. Set aside and repeat for the rest of the beef. The slices can now be used straight away or rolled up and stored in the fridge for a few days.

For the broccoli topping, trim off the stalks from the broccoli and cut into small dice. Blanch the florets in boiling salted water until they are slightly overcooked, then drain and leave to cool. Repeat for the diced stalks. Reserve a few small broccoli florets for decoration. Put the rest of the broccoli in a food processor and whiz until smooth, then season with salt and pepper. In a small bowl, mix the lemon juice with the olive oil. Take off the top sheet of clingfilm from the beef and season the meat with salt and pepper. Remove a quarter of the carpaccio slices and brush with the lemon oil. Spoon the broccoli purée on to a large serving plate and top with the brushed carpaccio slices. Decorate with the reserved broccoli florets.

For the caper and mayonnaise topping, arrange a quarter of the carpaccio slices on a large serving plate and drizzle over the mayonnaise, then sprinkle over the capers.

For the mayonnaise topping, arrange half the remaining carpaccio on a large serving plate and drizzle over the mayonnaise.

Lay the remaining carpaccio slices on a serving plate. Dress the rocket leaves with the olive oil and lemon juice and season to taste. Arrange the rocket on the carpaccio and top with the Parmesan shavings.

To serve, let everyone help themselves to the different carpaccios.

Steak and kidney pudding

Rognoni e manzo al vapore in crosta di strutto

This is a great version of a great British dish, which I borrowed from Bobby King at the Cottage Inn in Ascot. What makes it so special is the addition of a secret ingredient. No, it's not the Guinness, and it's not the tomato purée. Yes, you guessed it. It's the HP Sauce. **Tony**

Serves 6

1 tablespoon sunflower oil
1 large onion, thinly sliced
700g/1lb 9oz chuck steak, cut into
    2cm/^{3}/$_4$ inch cubes
225g/8oz lamb's kidneys, rinsed and
    cut into 2cm/^{3}/$_4$ inch cubes
3 tablespoons plain flour
350ml/12fl oz beef stock
250ml/9fl oz Guinness or ale
1 tablespoon HP sauce
1 tablespoon Worcestershire sauce

1 tablespoon tomato purée
1 teaspoon chopped thyme
large knob of butter
sea salt and freshly ground black
    pepper

For the pastry:
450g/1lb self-raising flour
225g/8oz suet
pinch of salt

Heat the oil in a large saucepan, add the onion and cook gently for a few minutes. Toss the steak and kidney in the flour and add to the onion, tossing well. Cook until browned all over. Pour in the beef stock and beer, then add the HP sauce, Worcestershire sauce, tomato purée and thyme and season well to taste. Bring to the boil and simmer very gently for 1 hour, until the meat is tender. Remove from the heat and leave to cool.

For the pastry, place the flour in a large bowl and stir in the suet and a good pinch of salt. Mix in enough cold water to form a soft dough, using your hands towards the end to bring it all together in a smooth, elastic dough that leaves the bowl clean. Leave for 5 minutes. Cut off and reserve a quarter of the pastry for the lid. Roll out the rest on a lightly floured work surface into a large circle. Use the butter to grease a 1.5 litre/2^1/$_2$ pint pudding basin, then line it with the pastry and fill with the steak and kidney mixture.

Roll out the remaining pastry and cut out a lid from it. Brush the edges with a little water and place in position on the pudding, pressing the edges well to seal. Cover with a double sheet of foil, pleated in the centre to allow room for expansion while cooking, and secure with string.

Place the pudding in a large saucepan and pour in enough boiling water to come half-way up the sides of the basin. Cover the pan and steam for 40 minutes. Remove from the pan and leave to cool for about 5 minutes. Take off the foil and release the pudding by running a knife between the pastry and basin. Invert the pudding on to a serving plate, cut into wedges and serve immediately.

Insalata di spinaci e ricotta salata

Spinach and salted ricotta salad

Salted ricotta is available from Italian delis. It is different from normal ricotta because the salting and maturing process hardens the cheese, giving it a character rather like feta. The distinctive flavour of the ricotta brings the delicate spinach leaves to life. **Giorgio**

Serves 4

1 large red onion
3 tablespoons extra virgin olive oil,
    plus a little extra for cooking
    the onion
3 tablespoons red wine vinegar
large handful of baby spinach leaves

5 tablespoons Giorgio's vinaigrette
    (see page 243)
5 slices of salted ricotta cheese
sea salt and freshly ground black
    pepper

Preheat the oven to 200°C/400°F/Gas Mark 6. Wash the red onion but don't peel it. Rub it with a little olive oil and place in a small roasting tin. Cover the tin tightly with foil and roast for 1 hour, until the onion is soft. Leave to cool, then carefully remove the skin and slice the onion into rings.

Mix the red wine vinegar with 2 tablespoons of the olive oil and season with salt and pepper. Transfer to a non-metallic dish and add the onion rings. Cover and leave to marinate for about 1 hour, until ready to serve.

Toss the spinach leaves with the vinaigrette. Sit one or two of the onion rings on each serving plate and pile the spinach leaves on top, leaf by leaf, to give a 'flower' shape. Break up the ricotta slices and sprinkle them on top of the spinach. Drizzle with the remaining olive oil, grind over some black pepper and then serve.

Slow-roasted belly pork with apple sauce and baked cabbage

Pancetta di maiale arrosto lentamente con salsa di mele e cavolo al forno

Belly pork has a lot more going for it than the traditional roasting cuts. For a start, there is a nice flat expanse of rind to turn into much-loved crackling, while the layers of fat mean that the meat is virtually self-basting as it cooks. **Tony**

Serves 6–8

1.25kg/5lb piece of boned belly pork
2 carrots, sliced lengthways into
    quarters
1 large onion, thickly sliced
2 celery stalks, thickly sliced
1 large leek, thickly sliced
800ml/1$^{1}/_{3}$ pints chicken stock
600ml/1 pint white wine
sea salt and freshly ground black
    pepper

For the apple sauce:
6 dessert apples, peeled, cored and
    sliced
50g/2oz caster sugar
large knob of butter
juice of $^{1}/_{2}$ lemon

For the baked cabbage:
1 small Savoy cabbage
1 streaky bacon rasher
large knob of butter

Score the rind of the pork with a very sharp knife (a Stanley knife does the job well), being careful not to cut right through the fat to the meat. Place the pork in a large saucepan and cover with cold water. Bring to the boil and simmer gently for 40 minutes, then drain and pat dry well.

Preheat the oven to 200°C/400°F/Gas Mark 6. Place the carrots, onion, celery and leek in a large roasting tin and put the pork on top, skin-side up. Pour 100ml/3$^{1}/_{2}$fl oz of the chicken stock into the tin, place in the oven and roast for 10 minutes. Turn the oven right down to 140°C/275°F/Gas Mark 1 and cook for 3 hours. If the crackling browns too quickly, cover loosely with a sheet of foil.

For the apple sauce, place the apple slices in a saucepan with a few tablespoons of water, then cover and cook gently until soft and pulpy. Beat them to make a smooth sauce, adding the sugar, butter and lemon juice to taste.

For the cabbage, remove the outside leaves and trim the core. Cut out a small piece from the top of the cabbage and insert the bacon, butter and a little seasoning. Wrap tightly in foil and place in the oven with the pork for the last hour of cooking.

When ready to serve, remove the pork from the roasting tin and leave to rest in a warm place (if the crackling hasn't crisped up, raise the oven temperature to 200°C/400°F/Gas Mark 6 and give it another 5–10 minutes first). Place the roasting tin on the hob. Heat gently, scraping up all the caramelised vegetables and meat from the bottom of the tin. Add the white wine and simmer rapidly until reduced by half. Pour in the remaining stock and simmer for a further 5 minutes, pressing the vegetables to a pulp, to make a gravy. Strain though a fine sieve and adjust the seasoning.

Slice the pork, cut the cabbage into wedges and serve with the apple sauce and gravy.

Pappardelle ai fegatini di pollo, salvia e tartufo nero

Pappardelle with chicken livers, sage and black truffle

Some people, like my good friend Vincenzo Borgonzolo who owns the restaurant, Al San Vincenzo, in London, cook with a natural Italian accent. Whatever he cooks it's going to taste and feel Italian. Whenever I make something like this pappardelle dish with its honest Italian flavours combined with the luxurious aroma truffle, it reminds me of Vincenzo's wonderful approach to food.

The best time to buy truffles is in late autumn and early winter, when you'll find them in the larger food halls and Italian delis. Even without truffles, this dish tastes great. **Giorgio**

Serves 4

350g/12oz pappardelle
1 tablespoon extra virgin olive oil
6 chicken livers, cut into 1.5cm/
²/₃in dice
6 small sage leaves, chopped

1 tablespoon brandy
25g/1oz butter, melted
4–5 thin slices of fresh black truffle
sea salt and freshly ground black pepper

Cook the pappardelle in a large pot of boiling salted water for about 8 minutes, until *al dente* – tender but still firm to the bite.

Meanwhile, place a heavy-based frying pan over a high heat to warm up. Add the olive oil, then the chicken livers and chopped sage. Season, then stir constantly for a minute or so, until the livers start to colour. Add the brandy and, standing well back, set it alight with a match to burn off the alcohol but leave the flavour. Remove the pan from the heat and set aside.

Drain the cooked pasta (reserving a little of the cooking water). Return the chicken livers to a medium heat and add the pasta, with about a tablespoon of the cooking water. Toss well and stir in the melted butter.

Transfer to a serving bowl and scatter the slices of black truffle on top, if you have them. If not, it doesn't matter. Serve straight away.

Salt beef with carrots and mustard dumplings

Manzo al sale con carote e gnocchi di mostarda

To salt your own beef takes over a week, so it's far easier and much more practical to buy a pre-salted piece from your butcher (silverside works well), soak it first and then cook it slowly in the oven. This is like all my best childhood memories served up on a plate. **Tony**

Serves 6

2.25kg/5lb joint of salt beef
25g/1oz butter
500g/1lb 2oz baby carrots, trimmed
2 tablespoons sugar
1 tablespoon Worcestershire sauce
chopped parsley
sea salt and freshly ground black
    pepper

For the dumplings:
6 slices of white bread, crusts
    removed
1 teaspoon English mustard

Soak the salt beef in cold water for 24 hours, changing the water twice.

Preheat the oven to 150°C/300°F/Gas Mark 2. Drain the beef and place it in a close-fitting casserole with about 300ml/½ pint boiling water. Cover the casserole with 2 layers of greaseproof paper or foil so that the juices cannot evaporate, then cover with a lid. Place in the oven and cook for 3 hours, until the meat is so tender it is almost falling apart. Remove from the oven and leave in the casserole for about 20 minutes.

For the dumplings, break the bread into pieces and place in a bowl with the mustard and 150ml/¼ pint of the stock from cooking the beef. Season with salt and pepper and mix to a paste. Roll into small balls about the size of a walnut and set aside.

For the carrots, heat the butter in a saucepan, add the carrots, sugar and a ladleful of the beef stock and simmer, uncovered, for 15 minutes, until the carrots are tender and all the juices in the pan have reduced down to a syrup.

Bring a small saucepan of the salt beef stock to the boil, add the dumplings and simmer for 4–5 minutes.

Heat 150ml/¼ pint of the remaining stock with the Worcestershire sauce. Serve each person 4 slices of the beef with some carrots, dumplings and a ladleful of stock, and a little parsley.

Coniglio al forno con prosciutto crudo e polenta

Rabbit with Parma ham and polenta

This was inspired by a dish my grandmother, Vicenzina Tamborini, used to make when I was a boy. Rabbit and polenta are natural companions, and they work even better with the saltiness of the ham and the bitterness of the radicchio. If you can't find radicchio trevisano, use ordinary radicchio instead. **Giorgio**

Serves 6

6 rabbit legs, boned
12 thin slices of Parma ham
2 tablespoons groundnut oil
50g/2oz butter
500g/1lb 2oz lard, melted

125g/4oz polenta
1.2 litres/2 pints milk
2 heads of radicchio trevisano
sea salt and freshly ground black
**   pepper**

Preheat the oven to 120°C/250°F/Gas Mark $^1/_2$. Wrap each rabbit leg in 2 slices of Parma ham. Heat half the oil in a large shallow casserole and place the rabbit legs in it. Fry over a medium heat until they start to colour, then add the butter. Turn the legs over and cook for a further 2 minutes. Cover the legs completely with the melted lard, then cover with foil and cook very gently in the oven for 1 hour, until very tender.

Meanwhile, cook the polenta. Put it in a large jug so that it can be poured in a steady stream. Bring the milk to the boil in a large saucepan; it should half fill the pan. Add 1 teaspoon of salt and then slowly add the polenta in a continuous stream, stirring with a long-handled whisk all the time, until completely blended. The polenta will start to bubble volcanically. Reduce the heat as low as possible and cook for 20 minutes, stirring occasionally.

Cut each radicchio into 3 and season with salt and pepper. Brush with the remaining oil and cook on a medium-hot griddle pan, until wilted. Spoon the polenta on to 6 serving plates and put the rabbit legs on top. Add the radicchio to the side and serve straight away.

Spezzatino di pollo al limone con carciofi

Chicken stew with artichokes and lemon

This is a very old recipe that probably originated in Sardinia. What saves it from being just another nice, homely stew is the surprising tang of the lemon juice. Be sure to use unwaxed lemons. **Giorgio**

Serves 4

4 lemons
2 bay leaves
2 tablespoons white wine vinegar
2 globe artichokes
2 tablespoons olive oil
2 onions, finely chopped
1 garlic clove, crushed

4 chicken legs
a little plain flour, for dusting
100ml/3½fl oz white wine
250ml/9fl oz chicken stock
50g/2oz parsley, chopped
sea salt and freshly ground black
    pepper

Half fill a saucepan with water and add 1 lemon, cut in half, 1 bay leaf, the vinegar and some salt. Snap the stalks off the artichokes. With a paring knife, starting from the base of the artichoke, trim off all the leaves and then remove the hairy choke, until you are left with only a neatly shaped heart. Cut another lemon in half and rub the base of the artichokes with the cut side. Put the artichoke hearts in the saucepan of water, bring to the boil and simmer, uncovered, for 5 minutes. Drain and cut into quarters.

Grate the zest of the remaining 2 lemons and sprinkle over the chicken. Dust the chicken very lightly with flour. In a large casserole, heat half the olive oil, add the chicken and cook over a high heat for a few minutes, until a golden crust has formed. Season with salt and pepper, then remove from the pan and set aside.

Heat the remaining oil in the casserole and add the onions, garlic and remaining bay leaf. Cook for 3–4 minutes over a medium heat, until softened.

Raise the heat and add the white wine to the pan, stirring and scraping at the residue on the base of the pan and allowing the wine to bubble and reduce for a minute or two. Add the reduced wine, chicken and artichokes to the softened onion mixture and cook over a gentle heat, stirring frequently, for about 20 minutes. Add the chicken stock, cover the pan with a lid and braise the chicken very gently for about 30 minutes, stirring half-way through.

Just before serving, add the chopped parsley and the juice of 1 lemon, then adjust the seasoning.

Rhubarb bread and butter pudding

Budino di pane e burro al rabarbaro

Bread and butter pud is one of those childhood cravings that don't ever seem to go away. Here, I've taken the pudding from the fish! restaurants and given it a bit of a grown-up twist with the twang of rhubarb, but essentially it's still a good old B & B. **Tony**

Serves 6–8

600g/1lb 5oz rhubarb, cut into 2.5cm/1in pieces
200g/7oz caster sugar
300g/10oz thickly sliced white bread, crusts removed
40g/1¹⁄₂oz butter, softened

300ml/¹⁄₂ pint milk
1 vanilla pod, split open lengthways
4 eggs
300ml/¹⁄₂ pint double cream
icing sugar for dusting

Preheat the oven to 180°C/350°F/Gas Mark 4. Put the rhubarb in a saucepan with 50g/2oz of the caster sugar and 2 tablespoons of water and bring to a gentle simmer. Cook for 5 minutes, or until the rhubarb is just tender but still holding its shape, then set aside.

Butter the bread with the softened butter and cut each slice into 4 triangles. Place a layer of the triangles, slightly overlapping, in a 1.8 litre/3 pint ovenproof dish. Spoon over half the rhubarb and top with the rest of the bread, then spoon over the remaining rhubarb.

Bring the milk and vanilla pod to the boil in a saucepan, then remove from the heat and leave to infuse for about 10 minutes. Meanwhile, whisk the eggs and remaining sugar together in a large bowl. Stir the cream into the boiled milk and pour on to the egg mixture, stirring well. Pour the mixture through a sieve, over the bread and rhubarb. Press the bread down gently to submerge it if necessary.

Bake the pudding for about 45–60 minutes, until just set. Remove from the oven and dust with icing sugar before serving.

Tiramisu
Pick-me-up pudding

The original tiramisu ('pick me up') was created in the Sixties at the El Toula restaurant, just outside Treviso. It's a truly great dessert, but perhaps a little heavy for modern tastes, especially at the end of a big dinner. Here is a lighter version, served in crisp wafer baskets. **Giorgio**

Serves 8

4 eggs, separated
100g/3^1/$_2$oz caster sugar, plus 2
    tablespoons
500g/1lb 2oz mascarpone cheese
6 tablespoons marsala wine
250ml/9fl oz fresh black coffee
16 savoiardi biscuits (sponge
    fingers)
cocoa powder, for dusting

For the *cialde* (wafer baskets):
100g/3^1/$_2$oz butter, softened
100g/3^1/$_2$oz caster sugar
100g/3^1/$_2$oz plain flour
2 large egg whites

For the coffee sauce:
200ml/7fl oz milk
2 egg yolks
50g/2oz caster sugar
1^1/$_2$ teaspoons instant coffee

To make the *cialde*, put the butter and sugar in a mixing bowl and beat together until pale and fluffy. Sift in the flour and mix well, then stir in the egg whites. Cover and chill for 1–2 hours.

Preheat the oven to 170°C/325°F/Gas Mark 3. Line 2 baking sheets with baking parchment and spread 4 thin circles of the mixture on each one, each about 12cm/5in in diameter. Bake for 5–6 minutes, until golden. Take the discs off the paper immediately and gently mould each one over an upturned tea cup or small bowl so that it forms a basket shape. Leave to cool, then set aside.

To make the coffee sauce, bring the milk to the boil in a saucepan. Mix the egg yolks, sugar and coffee together in a bowl. When the milk comes to the boil, pour it on to the egg mixture, stirring constantly. Return the mixture to the pan and stir over a gentle heat, without letting it boil, for 2 minutes or until thickened. Remove from the heat and set aside to cool.

For the tiramisu mixture, beat the egg yolks and 100g/3^1/$_2$oz sugar together with an electric hand-held beater until pale and quite stiff. Add the mascarpone and beat until smooth, then whisk in the marsala. Place in the fridge. In a clean bowl, whisk the egg whites and 2 tablespoons of sugar together until stiff, then fold into the mascarpone mixture. Return to the fridge for 30 minutes.

Put the black coffee in a bowl, briefly soak the savoiardi biscuits in it, then remove and set aside. Spoon 2 tablespoons of the coffee sauce on to each serving plate. Dab a bit of the tiramisu mixture on the base on each basket to prevent it moving around and put it on the coffee sauce. Fill the baskets with alternate layers of the cream and soaked biscuits, breaking up the biscuits to fit and finishing with a layer of the cream. Dust with cocoa powder before serving.

Real sherry trifle

'Zuppa Inglese' a base di sherry

This is no short-cut sherry trifle, but the real thing in all its great British glory, right down to the home-made fruit jelly and proper old-fashioned custard. **Tony**

Serves 6–8

6 sponge fingers or slices of sponge
    cake
8 macaroons
150ml/¼ pint sweet sherry
300ml/½ pint double cream
1 tablespoon icing sugar
2 tablespoons toasted flaked
    almonds

For the fruit jelly:
500g/1lb 2oz mixed strawberries
    and raspberries

175g/6oz caster sugar
250ml/9fl oz water
300ml/½ pint fresh orange juice
6 gelatine leaves

For the custard:
200ml/7fl oz whipping cream
200ml/7fl oz milk
1 vanilla pod, split open lengthways
5 egg yolks
1 egg
3 tablespoons caster sugar

Arrange the sponge fingers and macaroons on the base of a 1.8 litre/3 pint trifle bowl. Pour over the sherry and leave to soak.

For the fruit jelly, set aside about 12 small strawberries and 15 raspberries. Place the remaining fruit in a large saucepan with the sugar, water and orange juice, bring gently to a simmer and cook for about 10 minutes, until very soft. Pour through a sieve into a bowl, pushing gently with the back of a spoon to extract as much juice as possible. Return the juice to the saucepan, discarding the fruit pulp.

Soak the gelatine leaves in cold water for 5 minutes and then squeeze out the water. Add the gelatine to the warm fruit juice and whisk in well, until the gelatine has completely dissolved. Add the reserved strawberries and raspberries, then leave to cool. Pour the mixture over the soaked sponge fingers and macaroons and place in the fridge to set.

For the custard, put the whipping cream, milk and vanilla pod in a pan and bring almost to boiling point. Remove from the heat, cover and leave to infuse for about 20 minutes. Beat the egg yolks, egg and sugar together in a large bowl. Remove the vanilla pod from the cream mixture, pour the cream over the eggs and mix together. Pour back into the cream pan and cook very gently over a low heat, stirring constantly, until the custard has thickened. Be careful not to overcook. Remove from the heat, strain into a bowl and leave to cool, covering the surface of the custard with a circle of greaseproof paper to stop a skin forming. When the custard is cold, pour it over the set jelly and return to the fridge to chill.

Whip the double cream with the icing sugar until it just holds soft peaks. Pile on top of the custard and chill once more, until ready to eat. Serve scattered with the toasted almonds.

Fish

When you cast a line or a net, you might not catch anything. But when you do, it's as if all your Christmases have come at once. **Tony**

tony

I've been fishing since I was a kid and I still get excited by it. Before I started to sell fish I was a fish cook, and now I own a chain of fish restaurants around Britain. So on my day off, what do I do? Go fishing, of course.

The great thing about fishing is the unpredictability of the whole thing. When you cast a line or a net, or a fishing rod, you don't know what's under the water. You might not catch anything. But when you do, it's as if all your Christmases have come at once.

When people ask me what I like best about fishing, they want to know if the exciting bit is watching the rod and seeing the bite, or actually feeling the fish on the line. The thrill is definitely about the take and the play of the rod when you're game fishing for trout or salmon. But with beach casting, it's different. You start off all relaxed and floating, without a care in the world, and then suddenly, from out of nowhere, you see that bite. That's the best thing in the world.

The great thing about fishing is the unpredictability of the whole thing.

giorgio

I hate fishing. I'm not a big fisherman like Tony. I especially hate all that waiting. Waiting, waiting, waiting. That's why I'm not a very good pastry cook. I can't stand putting something in the oven and then just waiting around for everything to happen. I'd be forever opening the oven door to find out how it's going. 'Is it ready yet?' I like action, I like to move with my food.

So no, I am in too much of a hurry to be a fisherman. To be honest, I get more of a thrill out of finding a wild mushroom in the forest. Now that's exciting.

I used to go fishing as a boy in Lake Maggiore, near where we lived in northern Italy. We used to go after *gobbino*, or sunfish, which are a good eating fish, a little smaller than perch. I remember going out with my grandfather one time and we found a *buca*. This is a hole on the bottom of the lake floor where the fish go to lie low during summer, to escape the heat. They just stay there all day, then come out at night to feed. All you had to do was put in your line and pull out a fish. Put in and pull out. Put in and pull out.

That's the sort of fishing I like. No waiting.

on fishing

on fish

Fashion has a lot to do with what fish we eat. In the Eighties, farmed salmon was all the rage. I always thought that was a pity, because it meant we were losing our seasons. In the old days, every ingredient had its time. For strawberries, it was June; Stilton was only ever properly ready at Christmas; and you had to wait until late spring for the start of the salmon season. But by the Eighties everyone was lapping up farmed salmon all year round.

Then we all went sea bass mad. It was sea bass for breakfast, sea bass for lunch and sea bass for dinner. By the Nineties, recession had set in and sea bass was tossed aside. Instead, we all started eating peasant food like cod, mash and lentils.

As the economy started picking up again, and Sir Terence Conran began to open his massive restaurants, the sea bass came back. Tuna was big, scallops were on every menu and langoustines became the new glamour food. Fish and chips made a comeback, too, although I'm not convinced that they ever really went away.

If I were picking favourites, I'd have to go for scallops. This isn't just because I grow them but because they really are the king of shellfish — more so, even, than lobster. The big scallops we get are like tournedos (small fillets of beef). You can cook them like a fillet steak, or even make scallop Rossini with a garnish of truffle and foie gras. The flavour of a scallop is like nothing else, but if you really want to get the most out of it, then eat it raw. Unbelievable!

Wild Scottish salmon is probably the world's most wonderful fish, and large sea bass is great too, with its clean-flavoured, snow-white flesh and distinctive silver-grey skin, which crisps wonderfully when pan fried or roasted. Halibut, too, is majestic, but it can go one way or the other. Only one out of ten halibut is really good, but when you get a good one it's magic, mainly because of the texture of the flesh. When you bite into halibut, it doesn't flake; instead it's chewy, almost like meat.

Then there is eel. The best meal I ever had was in Portugal at a beach bar called Antonio's. They had just had a lot of flooding in the area and the marshes were full of eels. So the old man got one of these eels, chopped a chunk off it and marinated it in olive oil, oregano and sea salt for two days. Then he just banged it on the barbecue. It was magnificent. The flesh was succulent and the skin all crisp and crunchy. Throw in a bottle of Vinho Verde and you're in heaven.

I love cheap fish. Baby red mullet is one of my favourites, but I like all small fish. I used to get a mixed bag of small fish from Tony sometimes, and it was wonderful.

Often I will call up a fish supplier and ask, 'What is the cheapest fish you have?' I don't mean bad-quality fish but good quality that happens to be cheap. If I'm lucky I might get some anchovies or sardines. A lot of people don't think of them as very exciting fish but they're wrong. You can do anything with them, and whatever you do they always reward you with so much flavour and character.

Mackerel is a great fish. I always have it on my menus as a starter. There are about twenty different ways I can serve it. I can cook it like a saltimbocca, with ham around it, or fry it and make up an *agrodolce* (sweet and sour sauce), or maybe just flash it in a pan with a bit of red wine, then whisk in a little olive oil to make a light vinaigrette.

I also love to cook predators, such as pike and zander. They're like the sharks of the rivers. Like Tony, I love eel, but I just can't sell it in the restaurant. It's a pity because when you cook it on the grill with a herb and breadcrumb crust, the flavour is absolutely amazing. Come on, everybody! Eat more eel!

giorgio

Mackerel is a great fish. I always have it on my menus as a starter. There are about twenty different ways I can serve it.

tony

For great fish, you have to go beyond the supermarket and find a fishmonger. You have to buy a whole fish, on the bone. It's the only way you'll get really fresh fish. I once asked the staff in a supermarket where the coley had come from and they said, 'Out the back.'

You have to make sure the fish is slimy to the touch – which means it hasn't been out of the water for more than a couple of days – that it's bright red under the gills, and that its eyes are bright and clear. And don't forget to smell it. A fresh fish has a pleasant smell. If it smells fishy, then forget it. It's too old.

If you want fillets, buy the whole fish and fillet it at home – or get your fishmonger to do it for you. Be nice and he'll pinbone the fillets for you and give you the head and bones so you can make a quick fish stock for the freezer.

Everyone says to wash your fish but I say not to, apart from any obvious messy areas like the gut. If you fillet your fish at home without rinsing it all over, you'll keep in so much more of the flavour, and you'll really get to know what that fish is about.

If you want fillets, buy the whole fish and fillet it at home – or get your fishmonger to do it for you. Be nice and he'll pinbone the fillets for you and give you the head and bones so you can make a quick fish stock for the freezer.

Recipes
Fish

Scallops with bacon and bubble and squeak

Risotto allo champagne con capesante

English fish soup

Zuppa di pesce

Mackerel escabeche

Insalata tiepida di gamberi e borlotti

Swordfish club

Fish and chips with mushy peas

Linguine alla polpa di granchio

Whole poached salmon with warm potato salad

Nasello in scabeccio e insalata di finocchio

Eels and mash

Coda di rospo in salsa di noci e capperi

Filetto di salmone all'aceto balsamico

Griddled tuna with rocket and tomato

Scallops with bacon and bubble and squeak

Capesante con pancetta e crocchette di patate e cavolo

As far as I'm concerned, scallops are the king of shellfish. This is a killer recipe that combines the lovely sea-fresh sweetness of scallops with the campfire smokiness of bacon, the tang of a gribiche-style vinaigrette, and the comforting texture of bubble 'n' squeak. **Tony**

Serves 4

12 large hand-dived scallops
12 thinly cut dry-cured smoked
    bacon rashers
sea salt and freshly ground black
    pepper

For the bubble and squeak:
500g/1lb 2oz leftover roast potatoes
250g/9oz any leftover cooked
    greens, e. g. cabbage, Brussels
    sprouts, spring greens
a little semolina or flour, for dusting
2 tablespoons vegetable oil

For the red wine vinaigrette:
8 tablespoons good-quality
    vegetable oil
3 tablespoons red wine vinegar
1 small hard-boiled egg, shelled
    and chopped
2 tablespoons capers, rinsed,
    drained and roughly chopped
2 cocktail gherkins, finely chopped
1 tablespoon chopped mixed
    tarragon, parsley and chervil
1 tablespoon extra virgin olive oil

Pat the scallops dry with kitchen paper, then remove the corals and set aside. For the bubble and squeak, finely chop the scallop corals and put them in a bowl with the roast potatoes and greens. Mash with a fork until the mixture begins to hold together and then season well to taste. Divide the mixture into four and shape into cakes. Dust lightly with semolina or flour and chill for about 10 minutes.

Meanwhile, make the vinaigrette. Whisk the vegetable oil and red wine vinegar together. Stir in the rest of the ingredients and season with salt and pepper. Set aside until ready to use.

Wrap a bacon rasher around the edge of each scallop and secure with a cocktail stick, then set aside.

Heat a frying pan, add the vegetable oil and fry the bubble and squeak cakes for about 5 minutes on each side, until golden and crisp. Keep warm until ready to serve.

Heat a ridged griddle pan until hot, put the bacon-wrapped scallops in it and cook until the bacon is golden all over, rolling the scallops over with tongs to colour it evenly. Then lay the scallops flat and cook for 1 minute on each side.

Put the bubble and squeak on 4 serving plates and arrange the scallops on top. Drizzle the vinaigrette around and serve.

Risotto allo champagne con capesante

Champagne risotto with scallops

For me, making risotto is as natural as breathing. It won't take too long for you to feel the same way. Basically the act of making risotto is divided into four main parts. First we start with the *soffritto*, which in this case is the onion cooked in the butter. Then comes the toasting of the rice in the butter. Next, the hot stock is added, with continual stirring to allow it to be absorbed by the rice. Finally, when the rice is cooked, comes the *mantecare*, when the risotto is rested off the heat for 30 seconds and the butter (and cheese in non-seafood risottos) is added. Remember that your rice should be *al dente*, and pearly looking. Otherwise it is just a rice dish and not a risotto. **Giorgio**

Serves 4

6 large, fresh scallops
1 litre/1³/₄ pints hot fish stock
75g/3oz butter, plus an extra knob of cold butter
1 small onion, finely chopped

350g/12oz superfine carnaroli risotto rice
125ml/4fl oz champagne
sea salt and freshly ground black pepper

Chop 2 of the scallops into 5mm/¹/₄in dice. Slice the rest of the scallops thinly, season lightly with salt and pepper and set aside.

Put the stock in a saucepan and keep it at simmering point. Melt the 75g/3oz butter in a large saucepan, add the onion and cook gently until softened. Add the rice and stir for 1 minute to coat it with the butter. Add the champagne and cook rapidly until it is reduced by half. Slowly start to pour the fish stock into the rice a ladleful at a time, stirring well. After each addition, allow the stock to be absorbed into the rice before adding the next ladleful, letting it gently simmer away and stirring all the time. When all the stock has been added and the rice is tender (this should take about 15–20 minutes), add the diced scallops. Remove from the heat and leave to rest for 30 seconds, then add the knob of butter and stir together well.

Season well to taste and then serve the risotto in warmed serving bowls garnished with the sliced scallops. The heat of the rice will almost cook the scallops on the way to the table.

English fish soup

Zuppa di pesce all'Inglese

This is actually a traditional French recipe but given a distinct English accent. The harissa, saffron and Pernod might be imported flavours but the fish I've chosen are very much local heroes, so it's more your 'fish soup' than your '*soupe de poisson*'. If you like, you can serve this with grilled baguette slices topped with melted Gruyère or rouille. **Tony**

Serves 4–6

3 tablespoons olive oil
1 onion, roughly chopped
1 small carrot, roughly chopped
1 celery stalk, roughly chopped
1 leek, roughly chopped
pinch of fennel seeds
small pinch of saffron strands
1 teaspoon harissa paste
1 tablespoon tomato purée
200g/7oz gurnard, skinned
    and roughly chopped
100g/3½oz red mullet,
    skinned and roughly chopped

300g/10oz whiting, skinned
    and roughly chopped
75g/3oz fresh brown crabmeat
3 tomatoes, skinned and chopped
75ml/2½fl oz white wine
1 tablespoon Pernod
1 bay leaf
1 small fennel bulb, roughly
    chopped
1.5 litres/2½ pints water
sea salt and freshly ground black
    pepper

Heat the olive oil in a large saucepan, add the onion, carrot, celery and leek and cook gently for 3–4 minutes, until beginning to soften. Add the fennel seeds and saffron strands and stir through for a minute. Add the harissa and tomato purée, then tip in all the fish, including the crabmeat, and cook gently for about 10 minutes.

Stir in the chopped tomatoes, white wine, Pernod, bay leaf and fennel. Season with a good pinch of salt and freshly ground black pepper, then add the water and simmer for about 30 minutes. Purée the soup with a hand-held blender or in a jug blender. If you prefer a very smooth soup, pass it through a fine sieve as well. Reheat gently, taste and adjust the seasoning, then serve.

Zuppa di pesce
Italian fish stew

Practically every region of Italy has its own recipe for a fish stew, from the *brodetto alla Vastese* of Abruzzo to the Genoese *buridda* from Liguria. This one, however, is my favourite. With its dried chilli, tomatoes and slices of crusty bread, it is similar to *cassola*, the famous Sardinian fish stew. **Giorgio**

Serves 4

50ml/2fl oz olive oil
2 sprigs of rosemary, finely
    chopped
1 sprig of sage, chopped
1 teaspoon crushed chilli flakes
1 red onion, finely chopped
2 garlic cloves, crushed
100ml/3½fl oz white wine
400g/14oz baby octopus, cleaned
    and cut into pieces
8 small squid, cleaned and cut into
    4 pieces each
200g/7oz plum tomatoes, roughly
    chopped

600ml/1 pint fish stock
24 clams
24 mussels
8 large peeled raw prawns
400g/14oz monkfish fillet, sliced
sea salt and freshly ground black
    pepper

To serve:
4 slices of Tuscan-style country
    bread
1 garlic clove, peeled

Heat the oil in a large saucepan, add the rosemary, sage, chilli flakes, onion and garlic and sauté over a medium heat for 5 minutes. Pour in the wine and simmer until it has completely evaporated. Add the octopus and cook for 10 minutes, then add the squid and tomatoes. Pour in the stock, bring to the boil and simmer for 15 minutes. Meanwhile, scrub the clams and mussels under cold running water and pull the beards out of the mussels. Discard any open clams or mussels that don't close when tapped lightly on the work surface.

    Add the prawns, clams, mussels and monkfish to the pan and simmer gently for about 7 minutes. Discard any mussels or clams that haven't opened, then taste and adjust the seasoning.

    Rub the slices of bread with the garlic clove and place them in 4 large serving bowls. Ladle the soup on top and serve immediately.

Mackerel escabeche
Escabeche sgombro

Both Giorgio and I are mad about vinegar-based sauces with fish, except he calls them *agrodolce* and I generally use the French term, *escabeche*. Basically they're pretty much the same thing. In this dish the vinegar cuts through the oily quality of the mackerel, leaving you with something that sings in your mouth. **Tony**

Serves 4

1 tablespoon sunflower oil
8 mackerel fillets, skinned
2 lemons, thinly sliced
1 orange, thinly sliced
2 tablespoons olive oil
1 garlic clove, peeled
1 bay leaf, torn
2 carrots, thinly sliced

1 large onion, thinly sliced
6 tomatoes, deseeded and cut into
    1cm/$^1/_2$ in dice
50ml/2fl oz white wine vinegar
500ml/17fl oz white wine
sea salt and freshly ground black
    pepper

Heat the sunflower oil in a large frying pan, add the mackerel fillets and cook for 30 seconds on each side. Remove from the pan, arrange in a shallow dish in a single layer and put the lemon and orange slices on top.

Put the olive oil, garlic clove and bay leaf in a saucepan and heat gently. Add the carrots and onion and cook for 2–3 minutes, then add the diced tomatoes and some salt and pepper. Pour in the white wine vinegar and white wine, bring to the boil and simmer for a few minutes. Pour this mixture straight over the mackerel; it should cover the fish. Leave to cool completely, then cover with clingfilm and leave to marinate in the fridge overnight. Bring to room temperature before serving, garnished with toast, if liked, and accompanied by potato salad.

Insalata tiepida di gamberi e borlotti

Warm prawn salad with borlotti beans

Prawns and beans make one of the great classic combinations of Italian cooking. Fresh borlotti beans are in season in the UK in July and August and taste wonderful. If you're in a hurry, though, open a couple of cans instead and this whole dish will take only a few minutes. **Giorgio**

Serves 4

16 large peeled raw prawns
2 tablespoons extra virgin olive oil,
    plus extra for drizzling
3 garlic cloves, finely chopped
2 red chillies, finely sliced
50ml/2fl oz white wine
sea salt and freshly ground black
    pepper

For the borlotti beans:
about 1.3kg/3lb fresh borlotti beans
    (you will need 450g/1lb shelled
    weight)
4 sage leaves
1 bay leaf
6 sprigs of parsley
1/2 celery stalk
1 garlic bulb, cut in half

Shell the borlotti beans and put them in a large saucepan. Make a bouquet garni by tying together the sage, bay leaf, parsley and celery with string. Add to the beans along with the garlic bulb, cover with plenty of cold water and bring to the boil. Reduce the heat and simmer gently for 30 minutes or until the beans are tender, then drain and set aside.

Butterfly the prawns by slicing nearly all the way through them lengthways and opening them out.

Heat a large, heavy-based frying pan, add the olive oil, then add the garlic and chillies and fry for a few seconds. Add the prawns and fry for about 3–4 minutes, until just cooked through. Add the white wine and ignite with a match to flambé the prawns (but not the curtains!). When the flames have died down, remove the prawns from the pan and set aside.

Add the drained borlotti beans to the pan and heat through, so they take on the garlic and chilli flavours. Return the prawns to the pan and toss everything together, then season to taste. Serve the prawns and beans liberally drizzled with good extra virgin olive oil and sprinkled with lots of freshly ground black pepper.

Swordfish club

'Club sandwich' di pesce spada

They say that the best way to judge a top hotel is to order a club sandwich on room service. I reckon if any hotel were smart enough to put this swordfish version on the room-service menu for their guests instead of the normal turkey and bacon variety, they'd never get them to go home. **Tony**

Serves 2

300ml/½ pint vegetable oil
100g/3½oz sliced smoked salmon
4 thin swordfish steaks, weighing
    about 50–65g/2–2½oz each
1 tablespoon olive oil
6 slices of Granary bread

3 tablespoons mayonnaise
100g/3½oz iceberg lettuce, chopped
2 tomatoes, thinly sliced
sea salt and freshly ground black
    pepper

Heat the vegetable oil in a small saucepan until it is hot enough to turn a small cube of bread brown in about 1 minute. Add 1 or 2 smoked salmon slices and fry for about 30 seconds, until crisp. Drain on kitchen paper and fry the remaining smoked salmon in the same way, then set aside.

Heat a ridged griddle pan until very hot. Brush the swordfish steaks on both sides with the olive oil and season with salt and pepper. Place on the hot griddle and cook for about 2 minutes on each side, until cooked through and slightly charred.

Toast the bread lightly on both sides. Mix together the mayonnaise and lettuce and spread it on 2 slices of the bread. Place these on 2 serving plates. Place the swordfish on top. Put the crisp smoked salmon and sliced tomatoes on 2 more slices of bread and place on top of the swordfish. Top with a final slice of bread and secure the whole stack with a long wooden skewer. Cut in half and serve, with crisp chips (see page 56).

Fish and chips with mushy peas

Pesce fritto, patatine e pure di piselli

At fish! we always use haddock for fish and chips but at Bank we go a little upscale and use halibut. Both are perfect for deep-frying because they keep their shape and retain a nice, dense texture. The double cooking of the chips guarantees the golden crispness that chip lovers adore. You don't have to do the mushy peas but personally I think they're the best bit. **Tony**

Serves 4

5 large potatoes (Maris Piper or
   King Edward)
vegetable oil for deep-frying
4 x 175g/6oz pieces of halibut or
   haddock fillet, skinned
seasoned flour for dusting

For the mushy peas:
25g/1oz butter

2 x 300g/10oz cans of marrowfat
   peas, drained and rinsed

For the batter:
200g/7oz self-raising flour
pinch of salt
250ml/8fl oz beer such as Heineken
juice of 1/2 lemon
1 teaspoon malt vinegar

To make the mushy peas, melt the butter in a large saucepan over a low heat and add the peas. Cover and cook over a very gentle heat for 40 minutes, stirring occasionally, then crush roughly with a fork.

For the batter, put the flour and salt in a bowl and gradually add the beer, whisking all the time to make a smooth batter. Stir in the lemon juice and malt vinegar and leave to rest for at least 20 minutes.

Peel the potatoes and cut them into 7.5cm x 5mm/3in x 1/4in chips. Rinse well to remove excess starch (this stops them sticking together when frying) and dry thoroughly on kitchen paper. Heat some vegetable oil in a large, deep saucepan or a deep-fat fryer until it is hot enough to turn a cube of bread brown in about 1 minute. Fry the chips (in batches so as not to overcrowd the pan) for 2–3 minutes, then drain on kitchen paper and set aside.

Dust the pieces of fish in a little seasoned flour, shaking off any excess. Dip them in the batter and turn until evenly coated. Carefully lower them into the hot oil and fry for 4–5 minutes, until golden and crisp. Remove from the pan, drain on kitchen paper and keep warm.

Raise the heat a little, return the chips to the pan and cook for 2–3 minutes, until golden and crisp on the outside and fluffy in the middle. Serve the fish and chips with the mushy peas.

Linguine alla polpa di granchio
Linguine with crab

One thing we have in the UK is a fabulous supply of really good crabs. Being an Italian, I can't help feeling that a good crab deserves to be in the company of some good olive oil, plus a little garlic and chilli. These are stupendous, classic flavours that make one of the best pasta dishes ever. **Giorgio**

Serves 4

400g/14oz linguine
4 tablespoons extra virgin olive oil
3 garlic cloves, finely chopped
2 large red chillies, finely sliced
250g/9oz fresh crabmeat

150ml/¹⁄₄ pint white wine
small bunch of flat-leaf parsley,
   finely chopped
sea salt and freshly ground black
   pepper

Bring a large pan of salted water to the boil, add the linguine and cook until *al dente* – tender but still firm to the bite.

Meanwhile, heat 3 tablespoons of the oil in a large frying pan, add the garlic and chillies and fry gently for a few minutes. Add a final tablespoon of oil and the crabmeat and toss with the garlic and chillies. Pour in the white wine and leave to simmer until reduced by half. Season with salt and pepper and stir in the parsley.

When the pasta is done, drain it and return to the pan. Add the crab mixture and toss together well. Serve immediately in warmed serving bowls.

Whole poached salmon with warm potato salad

Salmone bollito con insalata tiepida di patate

Is wild Scottish salmon the best fish in the world? Silly question. Of course it is. And the best way to cook the best fish in the world is to poach it whole in a court-bouillon (an aromatic poaching broth of herbs, vegetables and white wine vinegar). The trick is to simmer it briefly, then let it steep in the bouillon to complete the cooking process without overcooking the fish. You can use ordinary salmon, but it will only be great and not fabulous. **Tony**

Serves 6–8

1 large darne (cut through the bone) of wild salmon, about 2kg/4½lb
1 quantity of Tony's mayonnaise (see page 244)
sea salt and freshly ground black pepper

For the court-bouillon:
1 onion, quartered
1 carrot, quartered
1 celery stalk, roughly chopped
a few sprigs of parsley, including the stalks
1 bay leaf

4 black peppercorns
1 teaspoon salt
100ml/3½fl oz white wine vinegar
900ml/1½ pints water

For the potato salad:
600g/1lb 5oz Jersey Royal potatoes (or other small new potatoes), scrubbed
3 large hard-boiled eggs, shelled and quartered
3 ripe tomatoes, quartered
½ cucumber, thinly sliced

Place all the court-bouillon ingredients in a fish kettle and bring to the boil on the stove top. Carefully place the salmon on the rack and lower into the liquid. Cover and simmer gently for 2 minutes. Turn off the heat and leave the fish to cool in the stock.

Cook the potatoes in boiling salted water for 15–20 minutes, until tender. Drain and toss with the hard-boiled eggs, tomatoes and cucumber, then with a few tablespoons of the mayonnaise (if the mayonnaise is too thick, you can thin it down with some of the court-bouillon). Season well to taste.

Preheat the grill. Lift the salmon out of the poaching liquid and carefully peel away the skin with a knife, taking care not to damage the flesh beneath. Place the skin on a greased baking tray and sprinkle with a little salt and pepper. Grill until crisp, then snip into rough pieces.

Serve the salmon with the potato salad, a good dollop of mayonnaise and a little of the crisp skin on the side.

Nasello in scabeccio e insalata di finocchio

Hake in a bag with fennel salad

The flaky flesh of hake really suits the 'cooking in the bag' method, which steams the fish without breaking it up and imbues it with the flavours of the lemon and parsley. I very much like the idea of serving the fish with a hot vinaigrette of herbs and garlic – the vinegar seems to wake up everything on the plate. **Giorgio**

Serves 4

4 x 200g/7oz hake fillets, skinned
juice of ¹/₂ lemon
125ml/4fl oz olive oil
small bunch of flat-leaf parsley,
    roughly chopped
4 garlic cloves, sliced
8 sage leaves
1 sprig of rosemary
4 bay leaves

75ml/3fl oz white wine vinegar
sea salt and freshly ground black
    pepper

For the fennel salad:
2 fennel bulbs, very finely sliced
1 tablespoon olive oil
juice of ¹/₂ lemon
2 tablespoons chopped chives

Preheat the oven to 150°C/300°F/Gas Mark 2. Place each hake fillet on a large square of foil and drizzle over the lemon juice and a little of the oil. Season with salt and pepper and sprinkle over a third of the chopped parsley. Wrap the fillets in the foil to make 4 parcels, sealing the edges. Bake for 15 minutes.

    Heat the remaining oil in a small saucepan until very hot, then add the garlic, sage leaves, rosemary sprig, bay leaves, the remaining parsley and a pinch of salt. Slowly add the vinegar a little at a time, being careful not to let it reduce the temperature of the oil, and simmer for 2 minutes.

    For the salad, toss the fennel with the olive oil, lemon juice, chives and some salt and pepper. Arrange a pile of fennel in the centre of 4 serving plates. Remove the fish from the foil parcels and place on top of the fennel. Pour over the hot oil and vinegar sauce and serve immediately.

Eels and mash
Anguille e pure

As a fisherman, I've always admired the eel for its slyness and cunning. It is the fish world's Sheriff of Nottingham. As an eater, I just love its good, solid flavour and firm, unctuous texture. Practically every country in the world has a great eel speciality. This is a traditional old English dish, but with elocution lessons. By darne of eel, I mean a cross-section of eel cut through the bone. **Tony**

Serves 4

2 x 225–250g/8–9oz darnes of fresh
    eel
900g/2lb floury potatoes, peeled
    and cut into large chunks
2–3 tablespoons olive oil or butter
150ml/¼ pint milk, warmed
sea salt and freshly ground black
    pepper

For the marinade:
150ml/¼ pint olive oil
150ml/¼ pint white wine
2 garlic cloves, finely chopped
2 tablespoons chopped oregano

For the mustard beurre blanc:
1 shallot, finely chopped
60ml/2fl oz white wine vinegar
60ml/2fl oz white wine
4 tablespoons double cream
125g/4oz chilled slightly salted
    butter, diced
2 teaspoons Dijon mustard
1 teaspoon wholegrain mustard,
    such as Pommery
chopped oregano to serve (optional)

Make the marinade by whisking together all the ingredients with some salt and pepper in a shallow, non-metallic dish.

Run a knife down the back of the eel, cutting through the skin and just into the flesh. Then run the knife along both sides where the natural seams are, cutting a little further into the flesh this time. Add the eel to the marinade and turn to coat. Cover with clingfilm and leave to marinate in the fridge for 24–48 hours.

The day of serving, cook the potatoes in boiling salted water until tender. Drain well and mash roughly to break up the potatoes. Gradually add the olive oil or butter, then the warm milk, and continue mashing until the potatoes are smooth. Season with salt and pepper and keep warm.

Heat a ridged griddle pan over a medium heat. Remove the eel from the marinade and place on the griddle pan. Cook for 20–30 minutes on each side, until the skin is crisp and the flesh tender.

Meanwhile, make the beurre blanc. Put the shallot in a saucepan with the white wine and white wine vinegar, season with black pepper and boil until the liquid has reduced by two-thirds. Pour in the cream and bring back to the boil, then remove the pan from the heat, and add the butter all at once, whisking until smooth. Stir in both the mustards and some chopped oregano if you wish, season with salt and pepper and keep warm.

Remove the eel from the griddle pan. The fillets should now fall easily off the bone. If they don't, return them to the pan for a few more minutes. Serve each eel fillet with plenty of mash and the sauce.

Coda di rospo in salsa di noci e capperi

Monkfish with walnuts and capers

This is a great dish that I invented purely by accident. One day in the restaurant, I was making a sweet and sour (*agrodolce*) caper sauce, while at the same time we were making a walnut sauce to serve with garganelli pasta. One of the boys in the kitchen used the spoon he'd dipped in the walnut sauce to serve out the caper sauce. While I was busy telling him off I tasted the spoon, and I couldn't believe how delicious it was. But I didn't stop telling him off.
Giorgio

Serves 4

4 x 250g/9oz monkfish tails, skinned, or 4 thick monkfish steaks, weighing about 200g/7oz each
4 tablespoons olive oil, plus extra for drizzling
75ml/2½fl oz hot fish stock
50g/2oz wild rocket
2 tablespoons Giorgio's vinaigrette (see page 243)
12 caperberries, rinsed and drained
sea salt and freshly ground black pepper

For the *agrodolce*:
100ml/3½fl oz white wine vinegar
100g/3½oz white sugar
200g/7oz capers, rinsed and drained

For the walnut sauce:
100g/3½oz walnuts
1 garlic clove, finely chopped
75ml/2½fl oz olive oil

First make the agrodolce: put the white wine vinegar and sugar in a small saucepan and bring gently to the boil. Simmer over a low heat for about 10 minutes, until it has reduced by half. Meanwhile, put the capers in a food processor and blitz until finely chopped (or chop them finely with a knife). Add to the reduced vinegar and sugar and cook over a very gentle heat for about 30 minutes, until all the liquid has evaporated. Leave to cool.

For the walnut sauce, place the walnuts and garlic in a food processor and blitz until finely processed. With the machine running, slowly drizzle in the olive oil until it forms a thick, glossy sauce. Season to taste.

Preheat the oven to 250°C/500°F/Gas Mark 10. Pat the monkfish dry with kitchen paper and season with salt and pepper. Heat the olive oil in a large frying pan and brown the monkfish pieces one at a time, turning them until golden all over. Transfer to a roasting tin as they are done. Place the roasting tin in the hot oven for 4–6 minutes, until the monkfish is cooked through. Remove from the oven, cover with foil and leave to rest for 5 minutes.

Meanwhile, in a small bowl, mix together the *agrodolce* and walnut sauce, adding the hot fish stock as you mix. Toss the rocket leaves with the vinaigrette.

Spoon the *agrodolce* and walnut sauce into the centre of a serving platter and place the rocket on top, then the monkfish tails. Spoon over any juices from the roasting tin and give the whole lot an extra drizzle of olive oil. Scatter the caperberries around the plate and serve immediately.

Filetto di salmone all'aceto balsamico

Pan-fried salmon with balsamic vinegar

Good fish deserves to be shown respect, which is exactly what this recipe does. It is all about acidity and sweetness and their effect on that wonderful fattiness of the salmon. This is one of those combinations that always make me smile. **Giorgio**

Serves 4

4 x 175g/6oz salmon fillets
450g/1lb spinach
25g/1oz butter
drizzle of extra virgin olive oil
sea salt and freshly ground black
   pepper

For the balsamic dressing:
100ml/3½fl oz balsamic vinegar
½ teaspoon sugar
1½ teaspoons honey
1 teaspoon Worcestershire sauce
juice of ½ lemon
100ml/3½fl oz olive oil

For the balsamic dressing, put the balsamic vinegar, sugar, honey and Worcestershire sauce in a mixing bowl. Stirring constantly with a wooden spoon, add the lemon juice and then slowly add the olive oil. Season to taste.

Brush the salmon with a little olive oil. Heat a non-stick frying pan until very hot, then add the salmon skin-side down and fry for 4–5 minutes, until nearly cooked through. Turn the salmon over and cook the other side for 3 minutes. Remove from the heat, cover and keep warm.

Wash the spinach and place in a large saucepan with just the water clinging to its leaves. Cook over a gentle heat until completely wilted, then drain well, squeezing out excess liquid. Return to the pan, add the butter and oil, and stir until the butter has melted and the spinach is creamy. Season well to taste.

Divide the spinach between 4 warmed serving plates. Place the salmon on top and spoon 3 tablespoons of the balsamic dressing over each piece. Serve immediately.

Griddled tuna with rocket and tomato

Tonno alla griglia con rucola e pomodoro

This dish is so simple to make, so foolproof and so delicious, that it just might succeed in converting a steak-and-chips nation to a fish-and-salad nation. I can only hope. **Tony**

Serves 4

**225g/8oz very ripe baby vine-
    ripened tomatoes
4 x 200g/7oz tuna steaks, about
    1.5cm/²/₃in thick
2 tablespoons olive oil**

**4 handfuls of wild rocket
4 tablespoons Giorgio's vinaigrette
    (see page 243)
sea salt and freshly ground black
    pepper**

To make the salad, put the tomatoes in a large bowl with the vinaigrette. Mix together with your hands, crushing the tomatoes slightly. Leave for 10 minutes.

Heat a ridged griddle pan until very hot. Brush the tuna steaks with the olive oil and season with salt and pepper. Lay the tuna on the griddle pan and cook for 2 minutes on each side, until just charred. Remove from the pan and set aside.

Add the wild rocket to the tomatoes and mix, then divide the salad between 4 serving dishes. Top each with a piece of tuna.

Everyday food

If a friend suddenly drops in for dinner, you have only to open the fridge and a cupboard and dinner is on the table before you know it. **Tony**

giorgio

I hate going shopping for clothes, or Christmas presents. I just want to get it over with as fast as I can. But food shopping is different. I am mad about shopping for food. I just love it. Even in the supermarket I have so much fun. When I go shopping with my family, I am always half a mile behind them, reading all the packets and the labels. It's so interesting for me to find out where something has come from or what it's made of. But I do get into a lot of trouble when I finally show up and everybody has been waiting for me in the car for nearly an hour.

When we're in Italy, it's worse. There are so many beautiful food shops, I can't help myself – I always have to go in and smell and taste. It drives the kids mad. They say, 'Oh no! Not another food shop!' But what can I do? They are so beautiful – the shops, I mean, although the kids are beautiful too.

I don't believe in shopping lists. They're okay if you're buying toilet paper or washing powder, but not for food. My ideas for recipes don't come to me until I'm in the shop, looking at the produce. I can't decide what to cook if I can't see the ingredients in front of me.

The other day, I was in a greengrocer's and saw some amazing organic leeks. They were so beautiful, they *talked* to me. Honestly, they were talking to me. So I took them home and made a potato and leek soup and finished it off with some black truffle and they were still talking to me. They were absolutely delicious.

If people had more fun shopping for food, they would do it more often. In Italy we shop every day. When you talk to a stranger in Italy, you generally talk about food, because you know everyone is interested in it. In England they'll talk about the weather or football.

The good thing about shopping often, especially in delicatessens, butcher's and fish shops, is that it gives you a chance to strike up a relationship with a shopkeeper, and that can be a very valuable thing. Once a shopkeeper gets to know you, he'll tell you when something really good has just come in, or he'll save something for you. I love going into Monte's, one of my favourite Italian delis in London, because Fernando will always say, 'Hey Giorgio, look what I have for you!' It could be a new prosciutto, or cheese with *ubriaco* (grape must). That's what I call shopping.

tony

The best piece of advice I ever had about shopping came from Giorgio. He once said to me, 'When you're shopping you don't have to touch, you just have to smell,' and he's absolutely right.

This is one of the big problems about supermarkets. I'm not anti-supermarkets. They are now a fact of life – especially in the suburbs – and, rather than rail against them like something out of an old episode of *The Good Life*, I really think we have to accept them and make the most of them. They're great for cans, jars, olive oils, and that kind of thing, but when was the last time you walked into a supermarket and were overwhelmed by the smell of fresh fruit?

If you're lucky enough to have a good greengrocer's, fishmonger's, cheese shop or farmer's market nearby, then you should use them before you lose them. And remember, always, to breathe in.

The main thing when shopping is to be flexible. You might be having friends around, so you'll go shopping with a good idea of what you're going to cook. But you just know that that idea is going to be ambushed five or six times by the time you've walked around the market or supermarket. My advice is to go ahead and let it get ambushed. Give in to it, and be swayed by the things you see.

It helps to have a rough idea of the seasons. Buy produce that's in season and it will have a better flavour. Also it won't cost you an arm and a leg because it hasn't been flown in from Kenya or California. People tend to think that only fruit and vegetables are seasonal, but fish, meat and even things like olive oil have their seasons, too.

I don't suppose it will come as much of a surprise when I tell you that our storecupboard is very Italian in nature. Pasta and risotto rice are the two most important things, and there is always plenty of both. I always keep three different types of extra virgin olive oil, from the very best cold-pressed to an everyday cooking oil – although I have to admit I tend to use the very best even in our everyday cooking.

Garlic bulbs and whole chillies hang in strings like Christmas decorations at our place, and there is always cheese in the refrigerator – mostly Italian cheeses such as Parmesan, pecorino, Taleggio and fontina that I buy mainly from Marco's little cheese stall at London's Borough market. Then I have all the things you might expect me to have: canned beans, canned tuna, canned sardines, sun-dried tomatoes and great big jars of dried morel and porcini mushrooms.

About the only things in the kitchen that aren't Italian are a bottle of soy sauce and some packets of felafel mix. The whole family fell in love with felafel when we went to Israel for Christmas one year to escape the winter. We stayed in a great place on the beach and my son, Jack, and I built a huge chair out of sand. I'll never forget the sight of Jack sitting in that chair in the hot sunshine, eating a felafel. He looked at us with a big grin on his face and yelled out, 'This is the best Christmas lunch EVER!' The tide was coming in all around him, and it looked as if he was floating out to sea. So every time we make felafels now, we all just laugh.

giorgio

Garlic bulbs and whole chillies hang in strings like Christmas decorations at our place.

The secret of good home cooking is a well-stocked storecupboard. By that I don't mean jars of Beluga caviar, tins of lark tongues and giant packets of La Mancha saffron. Rather, I'm talking about the sort of storecupboard that means you're prepared for any emergency. If a friend suddenly drops in for dinner, before you know it you have only to open the fridge and a cupboard and dinner is on the table.

I read somewhere that the best way to stock up a storecupboard is to pretend that you're going to a holiday house for two weeks and you have to take what you need or do without. For me, the essentials would be olive oil, a couple of vinegars, pasta, rice and Chinese egg noodles. I have to have a good mustard, good mayonnaise, plus a few basic sauces such as tomato, Worcestershire and soy. Butter, milk, eggs and Parmesan, of course; a few herbs and spices; and a good stock of cans, from beans and tomatoes to anchovies, olives and tuna. You can't really compare canned tuna to fresh. It's a totally different product. You could confit fresh tuna for twenty-four hours and you wouldn't get close to the texture you find in the canned stuff, but it's still craving material.

Then you have to allow for a few personal preferences – important ingredients that make you happy. In my case, this means canned herring roe, flat mushrooms, pickled onions and pistachio nuts. There is always a loaf of bread around. Fry the mushrooms in some butter, toast the bread, and you have a feast. Add a little bit of herring roe and it's something else again.

With that little lot, you can feed the family without a problem. Throw in a nice piece of meat or fish, or some fresh vegetables, and you can feed the Queen.

Recipes
Everyday food

Spaghetti all' acciughe e tonno

Onion soup with cider and cheese

Penne con salsa alle noci

Chorizo sandwich with tomato salsa

Inzimo di calamari e ceci

Spanish omelette

Risotto con funghi

Prawn noodle soup

Bresaola di manzo al caprino

Panzanella

Mushrooms and herring roes on toast

Tuna and potato salad

Tortino d'amaretto e rabarbaro

Rice pudding

Insalata di agrumi

Spaghetti all' acciughe e tonno
Spaghetti with anchovy and tuna

This is storecupboard cooking at its easiest. Virtually all you need is a can of tuna and a can of anchovies plus a couple of tomatoes, and in a matter of minutes you'll have one of the classics of Italian cooking on the table. The great thing about it is that it tastes as if you've gone to a lot of effort. **Giorgio**

Serves 4

350g/12oz spaghetti
2 tablespoons olive oil
2 garlic cloves, each cut into
    quarters
4 anchovy fillets in oil, drained
250g/9oz canned tuna in olive oil,
    drained

50ml/2fl oz white wine
50g/2oz capers, rinsed and drained
2 tomatoes, diced
10 basil leaves
2 tablespoons extra virgin olive oil
sea salt and freshly ground black
    pepper

Cook the spaghetti in a large pot of boiling salted water for about 8 minutes, until *al dente* – tender but still firm to the bite.

Meanwhile, heat the olive oil in a frying pan, add the garlic and fry over a gentle heat for 3 minutes. Add the anchovy fillets and cook very gently until almost melting. Increase the heat and add the tuna. Toss for a few minutes, then add the white wine and let it bubble for a few minutes to allow the alcohol to evaporate. Stir in the capers and tomatoes.

Drain the pasta, reserving 2–3 tablespoons of the cooking water. Toss the spaghetti with the sauce, mix in the basil leaves and extra virgin olive oil and season to taste. Add a little of the cooking water if the pasta seems too dry, then serve. In Italy, you wouldn't put cheese on a pasta with any sort of seafood, even canned tuna.

Onion soup with cider and cheese

Zuppa di cipolla con sidro e Cheddar

If your home is like ours, then there are always a few onions in the cupboard. There are a lot of different onion soups in the world but I really like this one for its old-fashioned English feel. It's simple, honest and warming, and the cider kicks it along quite nicely. This is a good any-time-at-all dish. It makes a great starter, and a perfect, easy lunch dish. **Tony**

Serves 4

25g/1oz butter
6 large onions, finely sliced
300ml/$\frac{1}{2}$ pint dry cider
1 litre/1$\frac{3}{4}$ pints chicken stock
small bunch of sage

4 slices of day-old country-style
    bread
100g/3$\frac{1}{2}$oz mature Cheddar cheese,
    grated
sea salt and freshly ground black
    pepper

Heat the butter in a large saucepan until foaming, then add the onions and $\frac{1}{2}$ teaspoon of salt and cook gently for about 15 minutes, until the onions are very soft. Pour in the cider, bring to the boil and simmer for about 10 minutes, until reduced by half. Add the stock, then tie the sage together with string and add to the pan. Simmer for 30 minutes. Remove the sage, then taste and adjust the seasoning, adding a little salt if necessary and plenty of black pepper.

Toast the bread, then sprinkle each slice with the cheese. Place under a hot grill until the cheese starts to melt. Ladle the soup into 4 bowls and float the cheese toast on top.

Penne con salsa alle noci
Penne with walnut sauce

We used to have a fantastic walnut tree at home that produced so many nuts we could never eat them all. So Mum would blanch them and make this walnut paste, and we would have jars of the stuff to get us through the year. Unfortunately they put an electric line through our property and had to chop the tree down because it was in the way. It was one of the few times I ever saw my grandfather, Mario, cry. **Giorgio**

Serves 4

500g/1lb 2oz walnuts in their shells
100ml/3½fl oz olive oil
3 garlic cloves, chopped
1 sprig of rosemary
1 sprig of sage
juice of ½ lemon
350g/12oz penne

2 tomatoes, diced
50g/2oz Parmesan cheese, freshly grated
50g/2oz flat-leaf parsley, finely chopped
sea salt and freshly ground black pepper

Shell the walnuts and blanch them for 4–5 seconds in boiling water. Drain the nuts, then peel away the skins while they are still warm and discard. Put the nuts in a food processor with half the oil, the garlic, rosemary, sage, lemon juice and 100ml/3½fl oz water and process to a thick sauce.

Cook the pasta in boiling salted water for 10–12 minutes, until just tender. Meanwhile, heat the remaining olive oil in a frying pan, add the walnut paste and diced tomatoes and heat through gently. Drain the pasta, add to the pan and cook over a gentle heat for 1–2 minutes. Stir in the Parmesan and parsley, adjust the seasoning and serve.

Chorizo sandwich with tomato salsa

Panino di chorizo con una salsa piccante

We Brits are pretty proud of our bangers but it's hard to beat a Spanish chorizo, with its belt of garlic, smoked paprika and chilli. It's one of those sausages that turn into an instant meal as soon as you look at them. **Tony**

Serves 4

4 fresh chorizo sausages
8 thin slices of sourdough bread
50g/2oz rocket
juice of 1 lemon
sea salt and freshly ground black
    pepper

For the tomato salsa:
2 tablespoons olive oil
1 small onion, finely chopped
1 garlic clove, finely chopped
1 red chilli, finely chopped
400g/14oz can of chopped tomatoes
10 sunblush (semi-dried) tomatoes,
    finely chopped

For the salsa, heat the olive oil in a saucepan, add the onion, garlic and chilli and cook for about 5 minutes, until softened. Tip in the chopped tomatoes and sunblush tomatoes and cook over a medium heat for about 10 minutes, until the mixture has reduced to a thick paste. Season to taste.

Heat a ridged griddle pan until very hot. Slice the chorizo sausages in half lengthways and cook on the griddle, cut-side down, for about 5 minutes, until they are charred and the paprika-red juices and oil run out. Turn the sausages over and cook for 2–3 minutes. Set aside and keep warm.

Place the bread on the hot griddle, pressing it down on to the pan until it is golden and charred and has soaked up the chorizo juices (you will probably have to do this in batches). Remove from the griddle, spread the salsa over 4 slices of the bread and top with the chorizo. Toss the rocket in the lemon juice and place on top of the chorizo. Season with salt and pepper, then cover with the remaining pieces of bread. Serve immediately.

Inzimo di calamari e ceci
Squid with chickpeas

Dried chickpeas can be superior but the canned variety is still a good product. They've been canned at their peak, they're already cooked, so the acid is gone, and they are ready in a flash. The great thing about this dish is the combination of textures from the squid and chickpeas – they are similar but different. Be careful not to overcook the squid. It's only a matter of seconds between meltingly tender and something that belongs on the bottom of your shoe. **Giorgio**

Serves 4

2 tablespoons olive oil
2 garlic cloves, finely chopped
2 large red chillies, deseeded and
    finely chopped
225g/8oz cleaned baby squid, cut
    into rings about 3cm/1¼in
    thick

50ml/2fl oz white wine
400g/14oz can of chickpeas, drained
    and rinsed
20g/³/₄oz flat-leaf parsley, chopped
sea salt and freshly ground black
    pepper

Heat the olive oil in a frying pan, add the garlic and chillies and fry over a medium heat for 1 minute. Add the squid and fry for just a few seconds. Pour in the white wine and let it bubble for a few minutes to allow the alcohol to evaporate. Using a slotted spoon, remove the squid from the pan and set aside. Add the chickpeas to the pan and heat through for a few minutes, then return the squid to the pan. Stir in the chopped parsley, season to taste and serve. I like to accompany this with a slice of grilled country bread that has been rubbed with garlic and brushed with extra virgin olive oil.

Spanish omelette

Frittata alla Spagnola

Unlike French omelettes, Spanish omelettes aren't dainty, delicate affairs. They're hearty, rustic and satisfying, as at home on a tapas counter as on the lunch table. They're fabulous hot, but just as good served cold as part of a picnic or as a side dish for a barbecue. Traditionally the potatoes would be fried from the beginning rather than boiled, but my way makes the tortilla feel just a little lighter and healthier. **Tony**

Serves 2

450g/1lb new potatoes, scrubbed
2 tablespoons olive oil
1 large onion, sliced
1 large red pepper, sliced
1 garlic clove, crushed

4 eggs
2 tablespoons milk
1 tablespoon chopped parsley
sea salt and freshly ground black
    pepper

Cook the potatoes in boiling salted water until just tender, then drain. When they are cool enough to handle, peel and slice them.

Heat the oil in a small, deep frying pan, add the onion and pepper and fry gently for about 10 minutes, until very soft and beginning to turn golden. Add the sliced potatoes and the garlic and cook, stirring, for a further 5 minutes.

Beat together the eggs, milk, parsley and some salt and pepper. Pour the egg mixture over the vegetables, turn down the heat to the lowest setting and cook for about 8 minutes, until the mixture is almost completely set – keep checking the underside to make sure it doesn't burn. Using a fish slice, carefully turn the tortilla over, or, if it's a little tricky, place a plate over the pan, invert the tortilla on to the plate and then slide it back into the pan. Cook for a further 2–3 minutes, until golden brown underneath. Cut into wedges and serve.

Risotto con funghi

Mushroom risotto

When I was a boy, we used to pick kilos and kilos of porcini mushrooms (ceps) in the woods surrounding my home. Every day we would eat fresh porcini in some form or another. What we didn't eat, my grandmother would slice, lay out on muslin and leave to dry in the sun. Today, I always have dried porcini in the storecupboard, and I find that even just a few add a great depth of flavour when all you have at hand is a bag of cultivated mushrooms. **Giorgio**

Serves 4

15g/½oz dried porcini mushrooms
1 litre/1¾ pints hot chicken stock
50g/2oz butter, plus an extra knob
   of chilled butter
1 onion, very finely chopped
300g/10oz superfine carnaroli risotto
   rice
100ml/3½fl oz dry white wine
2 tablespoons olive oil

1 garlic clove, chopped
200g/7oz fresh mushrooms, sliced if
   large
25g/1oz parsley, chopped
3 tablespoons freshly grated
   Parmesan cheese
sea salt and freshly ground black
   pepper

Put the dried mushrooms in a bowl, pour over enough hot water to cover and leave to soak for 20 minutes.

Put the stock in a pan and keep it at simmering point. Melt the 50g/2oz butter in a large pan, add the onion and cook gently for 3–4 minutes, until softened. Add the rice and stir for a minute or so to coat it in the butter. Pour in half the white wine and let it bubble for a few minutes to allow the alcohol to evaporate.

Add a ladle of the hot stock to the rice then drain the porcini, squeezing out any excess liquid, before adding to the pan. Then start to add the remainder of the hot stock a ladleful at a time, stirring well between each addition until the liquid has been absorbed.

Meanwhile, heat the olive oil in a large frying pan over a medium heat. Add the garlic and cook for a minute or so, until translucent but not coloured. Add the mushrooms and cook for 2–3 minutes, until they give up their juices. Pour in the remaining white wine and let it bubble for a few minutes so the alcohol evaporates. Stir in the parsley and season with salt and pepper.

When the rice is tender and all the stock has been added, remove from the heat and leave to rest for 30 seconds. Stir in the mushrooms, knob of butter and Parmesan, then season to taste and serve immediately.

Prawn noodle soup

Zuppa di gamberoni e taglierini

We don't cook a lot of Oriental food at home but there's always a bottle of soy sauce and a packet of egg noodles in the cupboard for those emergency cravings. This soup is one of the kids' favourites, and works just as well with leftover roast chicken, or slices of roast duck from Chinatown. **Tony**

Serves 4

1.5 litres/2½ pints chicken stock
350g/12oz egg noodles
225g/8oz raw king prawns, peeled
1 large red chilli, finely chopped
    (optional)
2 tablespoons Thai fish sauce
    (*nam pla*)

2 tablespoons light soy sauce
juice of 1 lime
8 spring onions, finely chopped
175g/6oz chestnut or button
    mushrooms, sliced
bunch of coriander, roughly
    chopped

Put the chicken stock in a large saucepan and bring to the boil. Add the egg noodles and simmer for 2 minutes. Then add the prawns and the chilli, if using, and simmer for a further 5 minutes. Stir in the fish sauce, soy sauce and lime juice, then add the spring onions and mushrooms. Ladle into deep bowls and scatter with the fresh coriander. Brilliant!

Bresaola di manzo al caprino

Bresaola with goat's cheese dressing

When you're entertaining, this makes a great starter, but it also works just as well for a summery weekend lunch or brunch with the family. Bresaola is cured dried beef that is always served finely sliced – it is to beef what Parma ham is to pork, in fact, and is quite delicious. Naturally it is from Lombardy, the finest region in all of Italy. **Giorgio**

Serves 4 as a starter to share

50g/2oz soft fresh goat's cheese
3 tablespoons white wine vinegar
6 tablespoons extra virgin olive oil
4 handfuls of rocket

juice of ¹/₂ lemon
200g/7oz finely sliced bresaola
sea salt and freshly ground black
**   pepper**

Put the goat's cheese in a small bowl and mash with a fork to a semi-smooth consistency. Slowly mix in the vinegar and 5 tablespoons of the olive oil, without emulsifying them together too much. It should still be a bit rough – this isn't a fancy French dish but a rustic Italian one.

Lightly toss the rocket with the lemon juice and the remaining olive oil and season to taste. Place a small bunch of the rocket in the centre of a slice of bresaola and roll up to enclose the rocket. Repeat with the remaining rocket and bresaola.

Arrange the bresaola rolls on a serving plate. Served drizzled with the goat's cheese dressing and a good grinding of black pepper.

Panzanella

Tuscan bread salad

Because of panzanella, I don't think I have ever thrown a single piece of stale bread in the bin! The great thing about this Tuscan salad is that it goes well with just about anything – grilled fish, chicken, prawns, you name it – or you can just sit down and hog a whole bowl of it to yourself. **Giorgio**

Serves 4

1 small loaf of country-style bread (about 2–3 days old), cut into large cubes
1 small cucumber, roughly chopped
1 large red onion, roughly chopped
3 very ripe tomatoes, roughly chopped
5 tablespoons extra virgin olive oil

3 tablespoons red wine vinegar
2 tablespoons capers, rinsed and drained
1–2 teaspoons sugar (to taste)
12 basil leaves, roughly crushed
sea salt and freshly ground black pepper

Place the cucumber, red onion and tomatoes in a large bowl and add the bread. Mix well with your hands and season with salt and pepper.

Whisk the olive oil, red wine vinegar, capers, sugar and some salt and pepper together and add to the bowl with the basil. Give it a good stir, then cover and leave in the fridge overnight for the flavours to mellow. The bread should feel moist but not soggy.

Serve as a starter or salad, or with grilled or roasted meat.

Mushrooms and herring roes on toast

Bruschetta di funghi e bottarga arringho

This may sound a little weird but the whole thing comes together in a very sound, very English way. Herring roe has a fabulous texture and its deep flavour nicely punches up the earthiness of the mushrooms. **Tony**

Serves 4

20 soft herring roes
4 tablespoons plain flour
2 tablespoons olive oil
50g/2oz butter
4 large flat mushrooms, thinly
    sliced

1 lemon
4 thick slices of country-style bread
small bunch of flat-leaf parsley,
    finely chopped
sea salt and freshly ground black
    pepper

Toss the herring roes in the flour and season with salt and pepper, shaking off excess flour. Heat the oil and butter in a large frying pan and cook the herring roes for 2 minutes. Add the mushrooms and cook for 3–4 minutes, until tender and golden. Squeeze the lemon juice over.

Toast the bread, then top with the mushrooms and herring roes. Season well with salt and pepper, sprinkle over the parsley and serve.

Tuna and potato salad

Insalata di tonno e patate

This is what you might call a loosely reinterpreted salad niçoise, put together with the kind of ingredients most homes probably have on hand. You can arrange it casually on the plate for a rustic look or use a ring mould – such as an egg poaching ring – for a little bit of fancy foot-work in the presentation. **Tony**

Serves 4

225g/8oz new potatoes
125g/4oz French beans
4 ripe tomatoes
200g/7oz can of tuna in olive oil, drained
6 anchovy fillets in oil, drained and finely chopped
handful of mixed salad leaves

sea salt and freshly ground black pepper

For the vinaigrette:
125ml/4fl oz olive oil
juice of 1 lemon
1 garlic clove, crushed
1 teaspoon Dijon mustard

Cook the potatoes in boiling salted water until tender. Meanwhile, blanch the French beans in boiling salted water for 1 minute, then drain, refresh under cold water and chop finely. Cut the tomatoes in half, squeeze out and discard the seeds and juice and finely chop the flesh. Flake the tuna into a bowl and add the tomatoes, French beans and anchovies. Toss together well, seasoning with a little sea salt and plenty of black pepper. Mix all the ingredients for the vinai-grette together, season with salt and pepper and spoon half the vinaigrette over the tuna mix-ture, tossing lightly.

When the potatoes are tender, drain them and refresh under cold water. Slice finely and toss gently with enough vinaigrette to coat them lightly. Toss the salad leaves in any remaining vinaigrette.

To serve, arrange the sliced potatoes on 4 dinner plates and spoon the tuna salad on top. Or, for a fancier presentation, place a ring mould in the centre of a serving plate and spoon a quarter of the tuna mixture into the middle, pressing down well. Arrange a quarter of the potatoes on top, then remove the ring mould and repeat on the other 3 plates.

Serve each portion topped with the salad leaves.

Tortino d'amaretto e rabarbaro

Amaretto and rhubarb tart

Amaretti biscuits are a great storecupboard standby. Their delicately bitter almond flavour adds an instant Italian accent to all sorts of puddings. I often just crumble them in my hand over chocolate mousse or panna cotta, or serve them with a glass of Italian dessert wine. In this tart, the almond flavour is reinforced by Amaretto liqueur, which in turn contrasts beautifully with the rhubarb. **Giorgio**

Serves 8

1kg/2¼lb rhubarb, chopped
300g/10oz caster sugar
1 cinnamon stick
300g/10oz amaretti biscuits
175g/6oz butter, plus a little melted butter for brushing

90ml/3fl oz Amaretto di Saronno liqueur
3 eggs
40g/1½oz plain flour
icing sugar for dusting

Put the rhubarb in a saucepan with 250g/9oz of the sugar, the cinnamon stick and a few tablespoons of water. Simmer for 5 minutes, until tender. Remove the cinnamon stick, then tip the rhubarb into a sieve and leave to drain over a bowl overnight (the rhubarb needs to be very dry).

Put the amaretti biscuits in a food processor and whiz until finely ground. Add the butter, Amaretto liqueur, eggs, flour and the remaining sugar. Whiz to combine the ingredients well, then cover and leave in the fridge for at least 30 minutes.

Preheat the oven to 170°C/325°F/Gas Mark 3. Brush a non-stick 23cm/9in springform cake tin with a little melted butter. Spread half the amaretti paste in the bottom and leave to rest in the fridge for 10 minutes. Cover the paste with the drained rhubarb and then cover that with the rest of the amaretti paste. Bake for 30–40 minutes, until the top is firm and golden.

When the tart is cooked, carefully remove it from the tin and place on a serving plate. Dust with icing sugar and serve warm or cold.

Rice pudding

Budino di riso

Rice pudding is part of everyone's childhood. To paraphrase that old beer ad, it touches the parts that other childhood memories cannot reach. Every culture has its own version of rice pudding but the British one takes some beating. When you've grown up with something done in a particular way, nothing else will quite do the job. **Tony**

Serves 6

900ml/1½ pints full-fat milk
600ml/1 pint single cream
125g/4oz caster sugar
grated zest of 1 orange

150g/5oz pudding rice
pinch of freshly grated nutmeg
25g/1oz unsalted butter, diced

Preheat the oven to 140°C/275°F/Gas Mark 1. Put the milk, cream and sugar in a pan with the orange zest. Stir over a low heat until the sugar has dissolved and the milk has come to the boil.

Put the pudding rice in a greased 1.8 litre/3 pint ovenproof dish. Pour the hot milk mixture over the rice and stir to mix. Grate over nutmeg and dot all over with pieces of the butter.

Place in the oven and bake for 1³/₄ hours, until the rice is cooked and most of the liquid has been absorbed, stirring once half-way through cooking. Serve warm from the oven. Ah, bliss.

Insalata di agrumi

Citrus salad

I can't stand sorbets when they are served between courses in fancy restaurants – it's like a punch in the mouth. But this dish has the lovely, light, refreshing effect of a lemony sorbet at the end of a meal, with its mix of fresh and candied citrus fruits. **Giorgio**

Serves 4

2 unwaxed oranges
100ml/3$\frac{1}{2}$fl oz water
50g/2oz caster sugar, plus extra for
    dusting
1 clove

2 unwaxed blood oranges
2 unwaxed grapefruit
2 unwaxed lemons
2 unwaxed limes

Using a vegetable peeler, pare the zest off the oranges, being careful not to remove the white pith, and place in a pan with the water, sugar and clove. Bring to the boil, stirring until the sugar dissolves. Simmer for 4–5 minutes to make a light syrup, then strain into a bowl.

Pare the zest off $\frac{1}{2}$ blood orange, $\frac{1}{2}$ grapefruit, $\frac{1}{2}$ lemon and $\frac{1}{2}$ lime. If there is any white pith attached to the zest, scrape it off with a small, sharp knife. Finely shred the zest, then place in a small pan, cover with cold water and bring to the boil. Drain and repeat this process twice, to rid the zest of its bitterness.

Pour a quarter of the strained syrup into a small pan, add the blanched zest and simmer gently for 10 minutes. Strain the zest, then toss with some caster sugar until evenly coated. Transfer to a sheet of silicone or greaseproof paper and leave in a warm place to dry.

Meanwhile, peel and segment all the fruit and arrange on serving plates. Scatter the sugared citrus zest over the top, pour over the remaining syrup and chill before serving.

Hunting and gathering

'How are we going to tell his mother and father you shot your grandson?' she yelled. I haven't really got into hunting in a big way since then. **Giorgio**

tony

These days, it is easy to become totally cut off from the origins of the food we eat. The more affluent and the more sophisticated we become, the further we distance ourselves from the food chain.

For many of us, food has been reduced to something purchased pre-cut, pre-portioned and pre-wrapped from a supermarket shelf. Man has progressed from being a hunter-gatherer to a trolley-wielding shopping unit – although I'm not sure that 'progressed' is the right word.

I have always loved the outdoors, and I have always been fascinated by hunting – not just with a gun but also with a ferret or a falcon. I reared my first Peregrine falcon as a boy, from a white ball of fluff, and trained it to hunt. These birds are beautiful to watch, flying 300 feet above your head, wings spread to full span, just hovering, and waiting.

Nevertheless, I don't believe in hunting purely for the thrill of the chase. The idea of pitting your skills against those of a wild animal may be thrilling, but for me it's about having a brace of birds or whatever to bring home for the pot at the end of the day.

While I enjoy all sorts of hunting – pheasant, rabbits, partridge, and even wild boar in Hungary – for me, hunting's finest moment comes each year on 12th August (The Glorious Twelfth), with the opening of the grouse season. Or, I should say, from 12th August on, as I have never hunted grouse on the opening day because the birds are young and inexperienced. I normally wait until November, when they are wiser and faster. It's more challenging, and ultimately more satisfying. In a good year, older birds will have more meat on their breast, so it's also more satisfying when the time comes to sit down to dinner.

When I'm hunting in a group, I always feel I have a distinct advantage over the others because I know what that bird is going to taste like when it finally gets to the table. I already have the thrill of the end result in my head, and not just the thrill of the chase.

Man has progressed from being a hunter-gatherer to a trolley-wielding shopping unit…

giorgio

I'm not exactly your Crocodile Dundee type. In fact, I'm about as keen a hunter as I am a fisherman, which is not saying an awful lot. I think it might have something to do with the day my grandfather took me out hunting when I was little and wound up shooting me in the backside. He was eighty-two and his eyesight wasn't very good, so I think he mistook me for a hare in the bushes. A very big hare.

When we got home, my grandmother pulled all the shot out of my bum with her tweezers and gave my grandfather hell. 'How are we going to tell his mother and father that you shot your grandson?' she yelled. I haven't really got into hunting in a big way since then.

Even so, I can understand why people enjoy it. To my grandfather and his friends, hunting was like a tonic. They were all old men, yet when they were shooting they were as sprightly and happy as kids at a birthday party.

There must be something good about just being alone with nature, without having to talk to anybody or worry about ordinary, everyday problems. It's like a parallel universe. I get the same feeling riding my motorbike. Just being on the bike for a couple of hours, without a telephone, without hassles, without problems – that's one of the great luxuries of my life.

My idea of hunting in the country has more to do with berries or mushrooms than animals. I love porcini mushrooms, or ceps (*boletus edulis*). There is nothing like walking around in the woods for ages without seeing anything, and you're about to give up, when suddenly you see the rounded, glossy brown bump of a porcini and your heart goes boom, boom, boom. You know that when you see one porcini, there's sure to be others nearby. So your eyes dart this way and that, looking for more. But you don't yell out or anything, because you don't want anyone else to hear that you've found mushrooms. Otherwise they'll soon be around tramping on your territory. A mushroom discovery is something you keep very, very quiet.

Truffles are worse. If you go to Alba in Piedmont during the truffle season, the worst thing you can do is leave your car by the side of the road while you go off looking for truffles. They don't like the competition around there, so by the time you get back to your car, don't expect it to have wheels.

There may be over 100 edible species of fungi in the UK alone, but there are just as many that could bring you grief. So you have to be careful if you do your own mushroom hunting, and avoid eating anything that hasn't been correctly identified. Mind you, that also goes for supermarket shopping!

In the UK, we still hold to the quaint old idea that game should always be hung until it is 'high'. It was long believed that the only way to treat game was to hang it by the legs until the legs rotted through and it fell to the floor. Then, and only then, was it ready to cook. And when we did eventually cook it, we always cooked the life out of it.

The simple truth is that game tastes so much better when it's fresh. If you get a fresh pheasant shot that morning, take the breast off and grill it. I swear it will be the most tender, succulent piece of meat you have ever eaten. I prefer my game simply grilled or roasted, and I suspect that a lot of the more complex recipes for game have evolved as a way of disguising the true flavour of the meat involved.

We should all make a point of finding out the age of our game. Three months in a bird's life can make a world of difference. Its diet is also important. If you buy from a game dealer, ask what the bird ate. If it's been fed on corn (maize), it's going to have a great, full flavour. If it's been fed on pellets, it will taste of nothing – like commercially reared chicken, or worse.

The flavour of wild game is a very individual thing. It depends on where it has been and how much it has moved around. If you shoot two wood pigeons and one has just been feeding in a pea field while the other has been amongst the trees eating berries, they will taste totally different. That's the great thing about wild game – you never quite know what you are going to get.

If you shoot two wood pigeons and one has just been feeding in a pea field while the other has been amongst the trees eating berries, they will taste totally different.

game

I may not be too crazy about hunting game but I love cooking it and I love eating it. The best game I've ever eaten was when my grandfather brought home about twenty quails. We all helped to clean and pluck them, then we stewed them up together and poured the birds, the vegetables and the cooking juices over a batch of freshly made soft polenta. Beautiful!

The thing to remember as a cook is that game already has so much flavour and character that you don't want to introduce too many other things to it. The trick is to keep the flavour of the game itself as clear and uncluttered as possible.

We eat so much meat that tastes of nothing that I find it very special to eat something that actually tastes wild. Each game animal is one of a kind, with characteristics that are all its own.

In Italy, the entire animal is used, and nothing is wasted. If you shoot a wild boar, the lungs and heart go into a stew, the head gets stuck on the wall and the skin gets turned into shoes. Crafts such as these are the last vestiges of the traditional rural societies.

Whenever my mother was given six or seven pheasants, she would hang them for a day or two, then cook the legs slowly until very tender, shred the meat and use it as a filling for ravioli. The breasts would then be taken off and simply roasted in the oven, while the bones would go into a stock. So we would sit down to ravioli, a little soup, and the breast.

Grandfather went even further than that. If he shot some hares, he would cut the pelt into strips and use them as draught-excluders on the bottoms of doors. For me, it's of more interest to turn the hare into a fantastic sauce for pasta, to keep me warm at the table.

giorgio

Recipes
Hunting and gathering

Roast grouse with porridge risotto

Grilled pheasant breast with prunes

Wild duck with orange, grapefruit and beetroot

Risotto alle quaglie

Piccione ripieno arrosto con lenticchie

Wild mushroom tart with walnut pastry

Game terrine

Pappardelle alle lepre

Tortelli di patate con funghi porcini

Ravioli di fagiano

Grilled venison cutlets with red cabbage and apple salad

Rabbit wrapped in bacon with mustard sauce

Frutti di bosco con yoghurt ghiacciato

Wild berry summer pudding

Castagnaccio al rosmarino

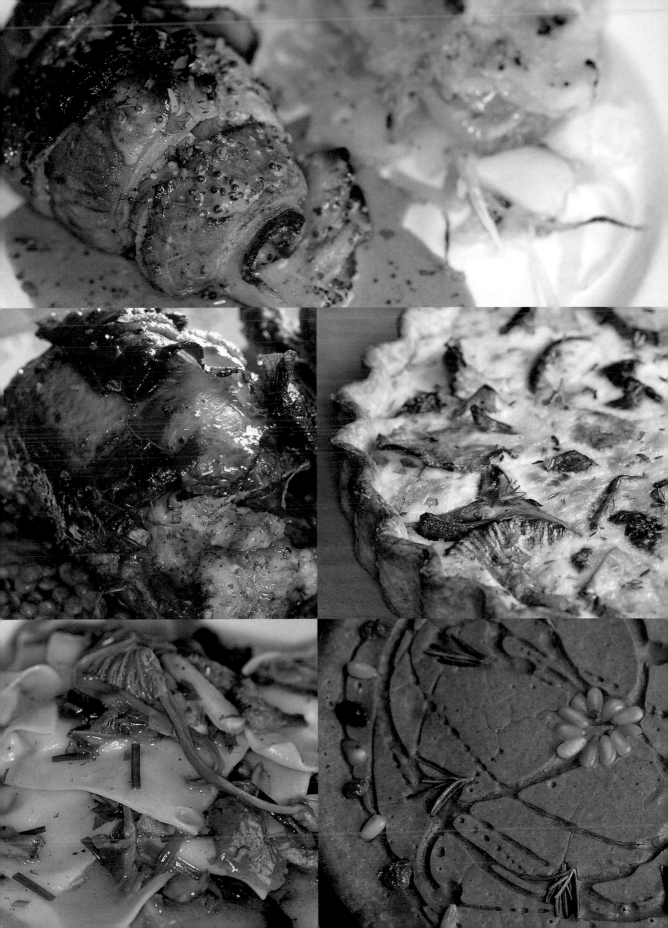

Roast grouse with porridge risotto

Pernice rossa arrosto con risotto di 'porridge'

The red grouse is totally Scottish in character, feeding only on heather, which gives it a wonderful flavour. So I thought it might be a bit of fun to take another of Scotland's famous foods – oats – and cook it in the style of risotto. Deglazing the pan with whisky means the gravy will have a wonderful Scottish accent, too. **Tony**

Serves 4

4 grouse (with their livers)
2 onions, roughly chopped
2 carrots, roughly chopped
8 streaky bacon rashers
4 sprigs of thyme
4 bay leaves
100ml/3¹/₂fl oz whisky
300ml/¹/₂ pint game stock or chicken stock
sea salt and freshly ground black pepper

For the porridge risotto:
50g/2oz butter
2 shallots, finely chopped
100g/3¹/₂oz porridge oats
500ml/17fl oz hot milk
50g/2oz Parmesan cheese, freshly grated
8 chicken livers, cleaned and chopped
the livers from the grouse, cleaned and chopped

For the parsnip chips:
3 large parsnips
vegetable oil for deep-frying

To make the parsnip chips, peel the parsnips and slice them very thinly, using a food processor, a mandoline or a U-shaped vegetable peeler. Heat the vegetable oil in a large, deep saucepan or a deep-fat fryer until it is hot enough to brown a cube of bread in 1 minute. Add the parsnip slices a few at a time and fry for a few minutes, until golden and crisp. Remove from the pan with a slotted spoon, drain on kitchen paper and sprinkle with sea salt, then set aside.

Preheat the oven to 200°C/400°F/Gas Mark 6. Put the grouse in a large roasting tin with the onions and carrots and season well with salt and pepper. Lay 2 bacon rashers over each grouse and put a thyme sprig and bay leaf inside the cavity of each bird. Roast for 20–25 minutes, until cooked through.

Meanwhile, make the porridge risotto. Heat half the butter in a heavy-based saucepan, add the shallots and cook gently until soft. Add the oats, then slowly stir in the hot milk. Cook gently for 5–7 minutes, stirring frequently, until thickened. Mix in the Parmesan and season to taste. Heat the remaining butter in a frying pan, add the chicken and grouse livers and fry until browned, then stir them into the porridge risotto. Keep warm.

When the grouse are done, remove them from the roasting tin, cover and leave to rest in a warm place while you make the gravy. Place the roasting tin on the hob and heat gently. Pour in the whisky and deglaze the tin by scraping up all the sediment from the bottom with a wooden spoon. Simmer until the whisky has reduced in volume by about two-thirds, then add the stock and simmer again, until reduced to a syrupy gravy. Strain through a sieve, then reheat and adjust the seasoning if necessary.

Spoon the porridge risotto into the centre of 4 serving plates and arrange the grouse on top. Pour over the gravy and serve with the parsnip chips.

Grilled pheasant breast with prunes

Petto di fagiano alla griglia con prugne secche

Plump pheasant breasts, Earl Grey tea, prunes and cabbage may sound like unlikely bed-fellows but it is amazing how every ingredient complements the other. Bashing out the breasts and marinating them in oil and herbs means that they'll only need a few minutes to cook, leaving them nice and tender. **Tony**

Serves 4

4 pheasant breasts
3 tablespoons olive oil
1 sprig of rosemary, finely chopped
2 sprigs of thyme, finely chopped
sea salt and freshly ground black
    pepper

For the sauce:
300ml/$^1/_2$ pint hot Earl Grey tea
100g/3$^1/_2$oz ready-to-eat prunes

25g/1oz butter
2 red onions, finely sliced
25g/1oz caster sugar

For the cabbage:
knob of butter
1 small Savoy cabbage, roughly
    chopped
zest of 1 lemon
150ml/$^1/_4$ pint double cream

Place the pheasant breasts between 2 pieces of clingfilm and bat them out to 2cm/$^3/_4$in thick, using either a meat mallet or a rolling pin. Place in a shallow dish, pour over the olive oil and sprinkle with the rosemary and thyme. Set aside for about 30 minutes.

Meanwhile, make the sauce. Pour the hot tea over the prunes and leave for 15 minutes to plump up. Strain the prunes, reserving the tea, and chop them roughly, then set aside. Heat the butter in a saucepan, add the onions and cook gently for a few minutes, until beginning to soften. Stir in the sugar and reserved tea and bring to the boil. Simmer gently for about 15 minutes, until the sauce has reduced by half and is thickened and syrupy. Stir in the chopped prunes, season with salt and pepper and set aside.

For the cabbage, heat the butter in a large saucepan and add the chopped cabbage. Stir well for a few minutes, until beginning to wilt, then add the lemon zest, cream and plenty of freshly ground black pepper and salt to taste. Simmer for 10 minutes, until the cabbage is tender. Cover to keep warm and set aside.

Heat a griddle pan until very hot, place the pheasant breasts on it and cook for about 3 minutes on each side, until scored and cooked through. Serve with the prune sauce and cabbage.

Wild duck with orange, grapefruit and beetroot

Anatra selvatica con arancia, pompelmo e barbabietole

Everyone knows duck *à l'orange*. This recipe takes the same idea but turns it into something wilder, tangier and far more colourful. The flavour of wild duck is a natural with citrus, and the beetroot turns the whole thing into party time. **Tony**

Serves 4

2 mallards
2 sprigs of thyme
2 large sprigs of flat-leaf parsley
600ml/1 pint hot chicken stock
3 pickled baby beetroot, diced
sea salt and freshly ground black
      pepper

For the sauce:
150ml/¼ pint orange juice
150ml/¼ pint grapefruit juice
50g/2oz caster sugar
300ml/½ pint chicken stock
3 oranges, segmented
2 grapefruit, segmented

Preheat the oven to 180°C/350°F/Gas Mark 4. Put the ducks in a large roasting tin and place the thyme and parsley sprigs inside the cavities. Pour over the hot chicken stock and cover with foil. Place in the oven and braise for 1 hour. Remove the ducks from the roasting tin and pour away excess fat, reserving it for later use (see An Englishman's Peking Duck, page 232). Increase the oven temperature to 200°C/400°F/Gas Mark 6. Return the ducks to the tin and roast, uncovered, for 35–40 minutes, until the skin is golden and crisp. Remove the ducks from the tin, cut off the legs and reserve for another recipe (ideally, An Englishman's Peking Duck, page 232). Cover the ducks with foil to keep them warm and leave to rest.

    Pour away all but 2 tablespoons of the fat from the roasting tin. Place the tin on the hob, add the orange juice, grapefuit juice, sugar and chicken stock and simmer for 15 minutes, until syrupy and reduced by half. Stir in the orange and grapefruit segments and simmer for a minute longer, then season to taste.

    Carve the duck breasts and serve with the sauce, sprinkled with the diced beetroot.

Risotto alle quaglie

Risotto with quail

A restaurant critic once took me to task for serving quail with risotto in this way, saying it wasn't correct. I was furious! This is the way it has always been done, and certainly the way I always do it.

When we cook risotto and quail, that's all we have. You don't serve accompaniments or side dishes. It is totally self-sufficient. **Giorgio**

Serves 4

4 quails
100g/3½oz butter
1 shallot, finely chopped
40g/1½oz pancetta, finely diced
125ml/4fl oz white wine
1 tablespoon tomato purée
900ml/1½ pints quail stock (made
    from the quail carcasses) or
    chicken stock

1 onion, finely chopped
300g/10oz superfine carnaroli rice
4 tablespoons tomato passata
olive oil for frying
4 tablespoons freshly grated
    Parmesan cheese
8 sage leaves, to garnish
sea salt and freshly ground black
    pepper

Preheat the oven to 170°C/325°F/Gas Mark 3. Cut the legs off the quails and bone each leg – to do this, run a very sharp knife along the length of the bone, then with the tip of the knife carefully ease the bone away from the flesh and remove it. Cut the breasts off the birds, too, and set them aside.

Heat 25g/1oz of the butter in a small casserole. Season the legs, then add them to the casserole and brown on both sides. Remove from the pan and set aside. Add the shallot and pancetta to the pan and cook gently until softened. Return the legs to the pan, pour in 2 tablespoons of the white wine and simmer gently until evaporated. Add the tomato purée and cook, stirring, for 1–2 minutes. Add 125ml/4fl oz of the stock and bring to the boil, then cover the casserole and transfer to the oven. Cook for 10 minutes.

Meanwhile, pour the remaining stock into a pan and keep it at simmering point. Melt 50g/2oz of the remaining butter in a large, heavy-based pan, add the onion and cook gently until the onion is very soft but not browned. Add the rice and cook, stirring, over a medium heat until it is coated with the butter. Pour in the remaining wine and simmer until it has been absorbed by the rice. Stir in the tomato passata and cook for 1–2 minutes longer. Add the hot stock a ladleful at a time, stirring well between each addition and waiting until three-quarters of the liquid has been absorbed before adding more. After about 10 minutes, add the quail leg mixture, together with all its liquid, then continue adding the stock as before.

Meanwhile, heat a little olive oil in a frying pan on a high heat. Season the quail breasts, add them to the pan, skin-side down, and sear for about 2 minutes, until well browned underneath. Turn them over and cook the other side for 1–2 minutes, then remove from the heat and set aside.

When the rice is tender and moist and all the stock has been added, remove from the heat and leave to rest for 30 seconds. Dice the remaining butter and stir it in, together with the grated Parmesan. Season to taste with salt and pepper.

Quickly fry the sage leaves in about 1cm/$\frac{1}{2}$in of olive oil for 30 seconds or so, until crisp. Put the risotto in 4 warmed serving bowls, top with the quail's breasts and the sage leaves and serve immediately.

Piccione ripieno arrosto con lenticchie

Stuffed pigeon with lentils

I learned how to make this dish from Mario Buonaccorsi, who at 62 was the oldest chef in my kitchen at Zafferano. Mario comes from Tuscany, where both pigeon and lentils are used a lot. The best thing he taught me here was to keep the stuffing simple, so it doesn't interfere with the flavour of the pigeon. **Giorgio**

Serves 4

4 wood pigeons
4 sage leaves
8 slices of pancetta
2 tablespoons olive oil
sea salt and freshly ground black
    pepper

For the lentils:
2 tablespoons olive oil
1 large carrot, finely diced
1 onion, finely diced
2 celery stalks, finely diced

150g/5oz green lentils
1 sprig of rosemary
1 bay leaf
¹/₂ garlic bulb
50g/2oz butter, diced

For the stuffing:
2 garlic cloves, chopped
50g pancetta, diced
small bunch of sage
50g/2oz butter
100g/3¹/₂oz fresh white breadcrumbs

First cook the lentils. Gently heat the olive oil in a heavy-based pan, add the carrot, onion and celery and stir to coat in the oil. Stir in the lentils, rosemary, bay leaf and garlic and add enough water to cover. Bring to the boil, then reduce the heat and simmer gently for about 40 minutes, until the lentils are tender but still holding their shape. Remove from the heat and season to taste, then leave to cool in their liquid.

    For the stuffing, process the garlic and pancetta in a food processor. Add the sage, butter, breadcrumbs and some salt and pepper and pulse until well blended.

    Preheat the oven to 180°C/350°F/Gas Mark 4. Stuff the pigeon cavities with the breadcrumb mixture, then tie the legs together with string. Place a sage leaf on the breast of each bird and cover with 2 slices of pancetta. Heat the oil in a large ovenproof frying pan, add the pigeons and cook for 2 minutes, until browned on all sides. Transfer to the oven and roast for 15 minutes. Pour off any excess fat and leave to rest in the pan for 7–10 minutes. Meanwhile, drain the liquid from the lentils and return the lentils to the pan. Add the butter and gently heat through.

    To serve, divide the lentils between 4 serving plates, place the pigeons on top and drizzle with the juices from the pan.

Wild mushroom tart with walnut pastry

Torta di funghi di bosco con pasta di noci

I'm not exactly your vegetarian type but this tart has so much going for it, and such a big, meaty, full-on flavour, that I don't feel as if I'm missing out on a thing. **Tony**

Serves 4

2 tablespoons olive oil
25g/1oz butter
4 shallots, finely chopped
2 garlic cloves, finely chopped
500g/1lb 2oz mixed wild
    mushrooms, such as ceps,
    girolles, trompettes de mort,
    chanterelles, picked over and
    gently wiped clean
2 teaspoons chopped thyme
grated zest of 1 lemon
small bunch of flat-leaf parsley,
    chopped
1 egg yolk
150ml/¼ pint double cream

100ml/3½fl oz milk
50g/2oz Parmesan cheese, freshly
    grated
sea salt and freshly ground black
    pepper

For the walnut pastry:
200g/7oz plain flour
pinch of salt
75g/3oz butter, diced
15g/½oz walnuts, toasted and
    ground
1 egg yolk
2–3 tablespoons water

To make the pastry, sift the flour and salt into a bowl and rub in the butter until the mixture resembles fine breadcrumbs. Stir in the walnuts, then gradually work in the egg yolk and enough water to form a fairly soft dough. Wrap in clingfilm and chill for 30 minutes.

Preheat the oven to 200°C/400°F/Gas Mark 6. Roll out the pastry on a lightly floured surface and use to line a 23cm/9in loose-bottomed tart tin, about 3cm/1¼in deep. Prick the base with a fork and chill for 15 minutes. Line with greaseproof paper, fill with baking beans and bake for 10–12 minutes. Remove the paper and beans and bake for a further 5 minutes, until very lightly coloured, then leave to cool.

For the filling, heat the oil and butter in a large frying pan, add the shallots and cook gently until softened. Add the garlic and then toss in the mushrooms and cook until they are beginning to soften and release their juices. Stir in the thyme, lemon zest and parsley and toss together, seasoning well with salt and pepper. Remove from the heat.

Whisk together the egg yolk, cream, milk and cheese and stir into the mushrooms. Spoon the mixture into the pastry case and bake at 200°C/400°F/Gas Mark 6 for 20 minutes, until set and golden. Serve with some dressed salad leaves.

Game terrine

Terrina di cacciagione

Any kind of game lends itself beautifully to pâtés and terrines. Here, I've combined the big, round, gamey flavours of venison and pheasant with the gentler pork and that lovely spread-able quality you get from chicken livers, and come up with the kind of terrine that works for just about anybody. Don't skimp on the back fat, as that is what will give you that nice, relaxed texture. **Tony**

Serves 6

100g/3½oz chicken livers, trimmed
    and roughly chopped
200g/7oz venison, roughly
    chopped
2 pheasant breasts or 1 small duck
    breast, skinned and roughly
    chopped
400g/14oz shoulder of pork,
    roughly chopped
350g/12oz pork back fat, roughly
    chopped

2 tablespoons brandy
100ml/3½fl oz cold chicken stock
50g/2oz blanched pistachio nuts
1 tablespoon sea salt
1 teaspoon freshly ground black
    pepper
10 rashers of thin, rindless smoked
    streaky bacon
1 bay leaf, torn into quarters
6 sprigs of thyme

Put the chicken livers, venison, pheasant or duck breast, shoulder of pork and back fat in a food processor and pulse until coarsely chopped (do this in batches if necessary). Tip into a bowl, pour over the brandy and cold chicken stock, then cover and leave overnight in the fridge.

The next day preheat the oven to 170°C/325°F/Gas Mark 3. Stir the pistachios, salt and pepper into the meat mixture. Line a 900g/2lb loaf tin or terrine dish with the bacon rashers, allowing at least 4cm/1½in to hang over the sides. Spoon the meat mixture into the tin, pressing it down well so it is compact. Lay the bay leaf and thyme sprigs on top, then cover with the overhanging bacon.

Place the tin in a roasting tin and pour in boiling water to come half-way up the side of the loaf tin. Cover with foil, place in the oven and cook for 30 minutes. Reduce the oven temperature to 140°C/275°F/Gas Mark 1 and cook for 1 hour longer, removing the foil 10 minutes before the end to brown the bacon. To check if the terrine is done, insert a skewer into the centre and press down on the top; the juices should run clear. Remove from the roasting tin and leave to cool, then chill for at least 24 hours before serving. It's good accompanied by country bread, gherkins, and a mixed salad with a walnut dressing.

Pappardelle alle lepre

Pappardelle with hare sauce

Pappardelle (wide ribbons of egg pasta) could have been invented just for this gutsy, winey, rich hare sauce. The way the sauce envelops the pasta is almost poetic. This northern Italian favourite cries out for a really good bottle of red wine. **Giorgio**

Serves 6

1 hare, cut into large pieces (you can ask your butcher to do this)
3 tablespoons extra virgin olive oil
1 carrot, chopped
1 onion, chopped
1 celery stalk, chopped
1 leek, chopped
1/2 bottle of red wine
2 tablespoons tomato purée
400g/14oz can of chopped tomatoes
1 bouquet garni
1 litre/1¾ pints hare, veal or chicken stock
500g/1lb 2oz pappardelle
small knob of butter

sea salt and freshly ground black pepper
freshly grated Parmesan cheese, to serve

For the marinade:
1 carrot, chopped
1 onion, chopped
1 celery stalk, chopped
20 sage leaves
1 sprig of rosemary
2 bay leaves
4 juniper berries
4 black peppercorns
2 bottles of red wine

Put the hare pieces in a large, non-metallic container with all the marinade ingredients, then cover and leave to marinate in the fridge for at least 24 hours.

Preheat the oven to 150°C/300°F/Gas Mark 2. Drain the hare and discard the marinade, then pat the hare dry with kitchen paper. Heat 2 tablespoons of the olive oil in a large flame-proof casserole, add the carrot, onion, celery and leek and sweat over a gentle heat for 3–4 minutes. Season the hare with salt and pepper and add to the pan. Cook over a medium heat until browned all over. Pour in the wine and bubble until nearly all the liquid has evaporated.

Put the tomato purée and canned tomatoes in a blender or food processor and blitz until smooth, then add to the pan. Cook for 5 minutes, add the bouquet garni and stock and bring to the boil. Cover, transfer to the oven and cook for 2–3 hours, until the meat is very tender and falling off the bone. Remove from the oven and allow to cool slightly.

Remove the hare from the casserole and set aside. Remove and discard the bouquet garni, then pass the sauce through a vegetable mill or sieve into a clean saucepan. Remove the meat from the bones, shred it into small pieces and add to the sauce. Check and adjust the seasoning.

Cook the pappardelle in a large pot of boiling salted water for about 8 minutes, until al dente – tender but still firm to the bite. Meanwhile, gently reheat the hare in its sauce, adding the knob of butter and the remaining olive oil. Drain the pasta and toss with the sauce. Serve with freshly grated Parmesan.

Tortelli di patate con funghi porcini

Potato tortelli with wild mushrooms

The idea for these tortelli comes from an old Lombardy recipe that I have experimented with a little bit. When I came to England I fell in love with the Jersey Royal potatoes here. They have such a fabulous flavour and special texture that they are a natural for the stuffing. The combination of the plump, almost bland tortelli and the big, gutsy, earthy mushroom sauce is what eating is all about. **Giorgio**

Serves 4–6

For the pasta:
500g/1lb 2oz Italian 'oo' flour
pinch of salt
1 egg
5 egg yolks
a little beaten egg for brushing

For the filling:
350g/12oz Jersey Royal potatoes, scrubbed
100g/3$\frac{1}{2}$oz butter
1 sprig of rosemary
25g/1oz Parmesan cheese, freshly grated
pinch of salt

For the sauce:
300g/10oz mixed wild mushrooms
2 tablespoons olive oil
3 garlic cloves, crushed
125ml/4fl oz white wine
1 tablespoon chopped chives
1 tablespoon chopped parsley
200ml/7fl oz hot chicken stock (see page 241)
50g/2oz butter
25–50g/1–2oz Parmesan cheese, freshly grated

First make the pasta dough. Sift the flour and salt into a food processor, then slowly pour in the egg and egg yolks through the feed tube, with the machine running. As soon as the mixture comes together into a dough, switch off the machine. Put the dough on a lightly floured work surface and knead for 10–15 minutes, until smooth and elastic, then wrap in clingfilm and chill for 1 hour.

To make the filling, cook the potatoes in boiling salted water until tender. Meanwhile, melt the butter in a small pan and add the rosemary sprig. Leave to infuse over a gentle heat for a few minutes, until the butter starts to colour, then set aside. Once the potatoes are cooked, drain and peel them, keeping them as warm as possible. Transfer the potatoes to a food processor and whiz until smooth, slowly pouring in the butter. Add the Parmesan and salt, then set aside to cool.

To make the tortelli, cut the pasta dough in half and flatten it slightly with a rolling pin. Pass each piece through a pasta machine on the widest setting, then fold in half and

repeat, each time switching the machine to a finer setting, until the pasta is about 0.5mm thick. Lay one of the pasta sheets on a work surface and place heaped teaspoons of the pota-to filling about 4cm/1½in apart all over it. Brush the other pasta sheet with beaten egg and lay it, egg-side down, on top of the filled sheet. Press the pasta sheets together around the filling and cut out the ravioli with a round pastry cutter or a knife, depending which shape you prefer. Cover with clingfilm and chill until ready to use.

To make the sauce, pick over the mushrooms, brushing off leaves or bits of earth with a pastry brush. Trim the stalks and tear the mushrooms lengthways into either halves, quarters or eighths, depending on their size, so that the stalks remain attached to the cups. Heat the olive oil in a frying pan and cook the garlic for a minute or so, then add the mush-rooms and cook for a further 2 minutes. Pour in the wine and bubble for a few minutes to allow the alcohol to evaporate. Stir in the chives and parsley. Keep warm over a low heat.

Cook the tortelli in a large pan of boiling salted water for 2–3 minutes, until tender, then drain and return to the pan. Gently stir the tortelli together with the mushrooms, hot chick-en stock, butter and Parmesan. Divide between warm serving bowls and serve immediately.

Ravioli di fagiano

Pheasant ravioli

Pheasant is popular all over Italy. It is generally made into a casserole, or roasted in much the same way as the French would prepare it. For me, however, it makes the perfect ravioli filling, with its subtle gaminess and rich flavour. **Giorgio**

Serves 4–6

3 pheasants
2 tablespoons extra virgin olive oil
100g/3½oz pancetta, thickly sliced
2 shallots, finely chopped
200ml/7fl oz white wine
50g/2oz fresh white breadcrumbs
4 tablespoons double cream
100g/3½oz Parmesan cheese,
    freshly grated

pinch of freshly grated nutmeg
1 quantity of Giorgio's pasta dough
    (see page 244)
large knob of butter
1 sprig of rosemary, finely chopped
sea salt and freshly ground black
    pepper

Preheat the oven to 180°C/350°F/Gas Mark 4. Cut the breasts and legs off the pheasants, then cut the breasts in half and bone the legs (you could use the carcasses and drumsticks to make stock for the freezer). Heat the oil in 2 large roasting tins set over the hob. Add the pheasant breasts and legs, skin-side down, and the pancetta and cook for 3–4 minutes, until nicely browned on both sides. Add the shallots and cook for a further 3–4 minutes, until softened. Pour in the wine, scraping up any residue from the base of the pan with a wooden spoon, and simmer until it has reduced by half. Transfer the roasting tins to the oven and cook for 5 minutes, until the meat is just done. Strain the juices and set aside 150ml/¼ pint for the sauce.

Before the meat cools, pass it twice through a medium-set mincer, or chop it very finely. Mix with the breadcrumbs, cream, Parmesan, nutmeg and a little salt and pepper.

Cut the pasta dough into quarters and pass each piece through a pasta machine on the widest setting, then fold it in half and repeat, each time switching the machine down a setting, and dusting with flour if necessary, until you reach the finest setting. If you are rolling the dough by hand, aim for a thickness of 1–2 mm. Cut into rounds with a 7.5cm/3in pastry cutter.

Divide the filling between half the rounds, brush the edges with a little water and place another round on top. Squeeze the edges together to enclose the filling – try and exclude as much air as possible.

Cook the ravioli in a large pan of gently simmering salted water for about 4 minutes, until just done, then drain well.

Meanwhile, melt the knob of butter in a pan, stir in the chopped rosemary and cook for 1 minute. Whisk in the reserved pheasant juices until well blended, then toss with the cooked pasta. Divide between warmed bowls and serve immediately.

Grilled venison cutlets with red cabbage and apple salad

Cotolette di cervo alla griglia con un insalata di cavolo rosso e mele

I think venison has more flavour, more interest and more substance than even your best, top-of-the-range, aged steak. The trick is to marinate it and not to overcook it, as it can start to get boring at anything over medium rare. If I'm cooking on the barbecue, I'll always add some rosemary sprigs to the hot coals, so the rosemary smoke can wrap itself around the meat. I can't think of a better way to toffee up the whole barbecue experience. **Tony**

Serves 4

8 venison cutlets, weighing about 75g/3oz each

For the marinade:
300ml/½ pint red wine
100ml/3½fl oz olive oil
4 sprigs of thyme
small bunch of flat-leaf parsley, roughly chopped
8 black peppercorns, crushed
6 juniper berries, crushed

For the red cabbage and apple salad:
1 small red cabbage
2 dessert apples, peeled, cored and diced
4 tablespoons red wine vinegar
6 tablespoons olive oil
small bunch of flat-leaf parsley
sea salt and freshly ground black pepper

Place the venison cutlets in a shallow dish in a single layer. Mix together all the ingredients for the marinade, pour it over the cutlets, then cover and leave to marinate in the fridge for 48 hours.

Cut the red cabbage in half and remove the tough core. Slice each half into very thin strips and tip into a saucepan of boiling water. Simmer for 3 minutes, until just tender but still a little crisp. Drain and refresh under cold running water. Drain again and pat dry, then place in a large serving bowl. Toss with the apples, red wine vinegar, olive oil, parsley and seasoning.

Heat a barbecue until the coals are red hot, or heat a ridged griddle pan until very hot. Remove the venison cutlets from the marinade, place on the barbecue or griddle pan and cook for about 3 minutes on each side, until charred and cooked to medium rare. Serve the cutlets with the red cabbage and apple salad.

Rabbit wrapped in bacon with mustard sauce

Coniglio avvolto in pancetta con salsa di mostarda

While the technique is pretty much French, I can't help thinking of this as a typically English dish. The honey and mustard coating gives the rabbit a medieval feeling, with its combination of sweet, hot and sharp flavours. I'm also giving you the recipe for *pommes boulangère* (baker's potatoes), because they go so well with the rabbit. **Tony**

Serves 4

6 tablespoons wholegrain mustard
2 tablespoons runny honey
100ml/3½fl oz white wine
4 saddles of rabbit, boned
8 thin rashers of lightly smoked
    dry-cured bacon
150ml/¼ pint double cream
sea salt and freshly ground black
    pepper

For the pommes boulangère:
750g/1lb 10oz potatoes, peeled and
    very thinly sliced
1 onion, very finely sliced
75g/3oz mature Cheddar cheese,
    grated
200ml/7fl oz vegetable stock
3 tablespoons dry white
    breadcrumbs
50g/2oz butter, melted

Preheat the oven to 200°C/400°F/Gas Mark 6. Arrange some of the potatoes and onion overlapping in the bottom of a buttered shallow ovenproof dish. Sprinkle with some of the grated cheese and season lightly with salt and pepper. Repeat these layers until the dish is full. Pour over the stock and sprinkle with the breadcrumbs. Pour the melted butter over the breadcrumbs and cover with foil. Bake for 50 minutes, until the onions and potatoes are tender, removing the foil for 15 minutes before serving, to allow the top of the dish to brown.

Meanwhile, mix 4 tablespoons of the mustard with the honey and 1 tablespoon of the white wine to make a thick paste. Spread this over each saddle of rabbit and then wrap the bacon around to cover the paste. Place in a roasting tin and roast for 35 minutes at 200°C/400°F/Gas Mark 6, until the rabbit is done and the bacon is browned and crisp. Remove from the oven and leave to rest for 5 minutes. Take the rabbit out of the tin, cover and set aside.

Place the roasting tin on the stove top and heat gently. Pour in the remaining white wine and deglaze the pan by scraping up any sediment from the base. Allow the wine to bubble and reduce by half, then pour in the cream and add the remaining mustard, whisking together well. Season to taste.

Put each saddle of rabbit on a serving plate with a spoonful of the potatoes and some of the mustard cream.

Frutti di bosco con yoghurt ghiacciato

Wild berries with frozen yoghurt

To get the best flavour from this wonderful dessert, you really need to use berries that you've picked yourself on a warm summer's day – strawberries, blueberries, raspberries and, in autumn, blackberries. At home, I often use frozen summer fruits to make an instant berry sauce to serve with them. **Giorgio**

Serves 4

150g/5oz frozen summer fruits
100g/3½oz caster sugar
350g/12oz plain yoghurt
100ml/3½fl oz single cream

100g/3½oz strawberries
100g/3½oz blueberries
100g/3½oz raspberries
100g/3½oz blackberries

Place the frozen fruits and half a tablespoon of the sugar in a small pan and heat gently, stirring, until thawed. Place in a food processor and blend until smooth. Chill until ready to serve.

Stir together the yoghurt, cream and remaining sugar and place in an ice-cream maker. Churn for 20–25 minutes or until the mixture has frozen. If you don't have an ice-cream maker, pour the mixture into a shallow container, place in the freezer for 1 hour, then transfer to a food processor and whiz until smooth. Freeze for 2 hours, then process again, before freezing until firm.

Hull and quarter the strawberries and divide between 4 bowls with the blueberries, raspberries and blackberries. Spoon the frozen yoghurt on top, pour over the puréed sauce and serve.

Wild berry summer pudding

Dolce estivo con frutti di bosco

I still think it's something of a minor miracle that a few slices of bread and a pile of berries can turn into something so drop-dead gorgeous, so delicious and so, well, puddingy. You know summer is with us when this beauty hits the table. Of course, you can use cultivated berries, but if you can pick your own or get the wild variety you're in for a treat. **Tony**

Serves 4

900g/2lb mixed wild berries, such as wild strawberries, blackberries and blackcurrants
75g/3oz caster sugar

8 large slices of white bread (preferably a few days old), cut 5mm/$\frac{1}{4}$in thick

Put the berries and sugar in a saucepan with 3 tablespoons of water. Bring to a gentle simmer and cook gently for 3–4 minutes, until the juices begin to run. Remove from the heat and set aside.

Cut off the crusts from the bread slices, then cut a round of bread from one slice to fit the base of a 1.5 litre/2$\frac{1}{2}$ pint pudding basin and set aside. Cut the remaining slices in half lengthways, lightly dip them in the fruit mixture and arrange them around the sides of the pudding basin, overlapping them slightly at the bottom so they fit neatly and tightly together, and making sure there are no gaps. Put the round of bread in the bottom to cover the base. Spoon about 100ml/3$\frac{1}{2}$fl oz of the juice from the fruit into a jug and set aside. Fill the bread-lined pudding basin with the fruit and remaining juice and then cover the top with the remaining bread slices, trimming them to fit. Cover the pudding with a saucer that just fits inside the basin, then set a heavy weight (or a can of beans) on top. Leave the pudding in the fridge overnight.

To unmould the pudding, remove the weight and saucer, place a serving plate on top of the basin, then, holding both plate and basin, turn them upside-down, gently shaking the pudding on to the plate. Lift off the basin and spoon the reserved juices over the pudding to cover any pale patches of bread. Serve cut into wedges, accompanied by cream or vanilla ice-cream.

Castagnaccio al rosmarino

Chestnut pudding with rosemary

For anyone who grew up in northern Italy, this is the equivalent of the English bread and butter pudding. One bite and you're immediately transported back to your childhood. For non-Italians, it can be something of an acquired taste, because it has an almost medieval flavour and no sugar – just the natural sweetness of the sultanas and chestnut flour. **Giorgio**

Serves 4

100g/3¹⁄₂oz sultanas
500g/1lb 2oz chestnut flour
300ml/¹⁄₂ pint water

150ml/¹⁄₄ pint olive oil
50g/2oz pine nuts
1 rosemary sprig, finely chopped

Preheat the oven to 170°C/325°F/Gas Mark 3. Place the sultanas in a small bowl, cover with warm water and set aside for 15 minutes to plump up.

Sift the chestnut flour into a large bowl. Gradually whisk in the water, followed by the olive oil, to make a smooth batter. Drain the sultanas and stir them into the batter with the pine nuts and rosemary, reserving a few sultanas and pine nuts for decoration.

Pour the batter into an oiled 18cm/7in round cake tin and decorate with the reserved sultanas and pine nuts. Bake for 40–45 minutes, until firm to the touch. Allow the pudding to cool in the tin for 5 minutes, then turn out on to a wire rack to cool. Serve warm or at room temperature.

Alfresco

I think we're better at commuting through nature than communing with it. **Tony**

Eating outdoors is what people do practically all year round in much of Italy – especially in the South. Even in the North, almost every household has a little *terrazza* that is an extension of the kitchen, where you eat your meals for at least four or five months of the year. We lived in the country anyway, so the idea of going off on a special picnic to get away from it all didn't have the same importance attached to it as it does in London.

To us, eating outdoors was a natural part of our lives, not something you planned for days ahead. Nevertheless, there was one very special Tuesday every year when the whole family would set out to enjoy a spectacular picnic lunch. My grandmother would insist on making a pilgrimage to the sanctuary, or church, at Madonna di Oropa, near Biella, where the Madonna was supposed to perform miracles. For us kids, it was a wonderful time, because the church service was followed by a huge al fresco meal, where everybody would sit down on the grass around the church and eat enormous amounts of fantastic food.

My father would stop at a bakery in the town of Biella itself and pick up some giant grissini. When the time came to eat, the grissini would be laid out with some salami, along with all sorts of fabulous things that my grandmother had made. I especially remember her wonderful *vitello tonnato*. She would cook the veal first, slice it thinly, then stack the slices together on end, interspersed with the creamy tuna sauce. Then she would pour more of the sauce over the whole lot and put it all in a plastic container. So then, when you opened it and pulled out a slice of veal, all the sauce would come up with it. It was so good we all used to fight over who had the last slice.

Then there were big bowls of Russian salad (diced vegetables in mayonnaise), roll-ups of cabbage leaves with meat and breadcrumb stuffing, deep-fried courgette flowers filled with cheese, and all sorts of preserved vegetables – artichokes, olives and caponata, a Sicilian aubergine preserve. Potato salad was a very important dish too, especially the way my grandmother would make it. First, she would boil three or four ladlefuls of chicken stock until reduced to almost nothing, then she would add onion and vinegar and mix it all together with the potatoes.

But not all my outdoor eating was so special. The flavours I remember most are the honest, uncluttered flavours of simple food, enjoyed in the company of good friends.

I remember once when I visited the family of our friend, Enzo, in Liguria. We spent the day among the rocks on a very beautiful beach, and when we got hungry Enzo's father cut up a big loaf of bread into thick slices. Then he cut some fat, ripe tomatoes in half, which he squished about a bit with the blade of his knife. Then he squeezed them all over the bread, along with a little olive oil, salt and pepper. The flavours were alive in our mouths. No fuss, no pretensions. For me, that is outdoor eating at its best.

The British have a wonderfully romanticised view of eating outdoors. We all have this great picture in our minds of escaping to somewhere wild and green and getting back to basics, but I'm not sure we really know how to go about it. You only have to go out on a motorway in the height of summer to realise that. There's nothing sadder than the sight of your typically British family set up by the roadside with their fold-away table and fold-away chairs, desperately trying to commune with nature as the traffic flies past them. You'd think they were sitting in their own drawing room, expecting Auntie Mavis to drop in any minute. I think we're better at commuting through nature than communing with it.

I guess the weather is partly to blame. We simply don't have enough opportunities to go out and practise getting it right. At the first weak rays of summer sun, we rush about packing our wicker picnic baskets, filling up our flasks, getting the old picnic blanket out of mothballs and bundling the kids into the car as if there's not a minute to lose. Generally, we pack so much stuff you would think we were going away for two weeks' holiday and not just a day in the country. So much for getting away from it all.

We also tend to take the wrong sort of food with us on picnics. When you look at the elegant comestibles the Victorians used to take with them, with their moulded this and jellied that, by the time they finally got it all on the road it was probably time to come back home again. Where's the point in that?

A picnic is not just an indoor meal taken outdoors. You really have to leave your meat-and-two-veg mentality at home and pare down the whole eating experience to its essentials. This shouldn't be too hard. After all, we British have already invented some of the best picnic food in the world. Take your Scotch egg, for example. Here you have a totally self-contained, fully functional, crumbed picnic kit, ready to go. Throw in a jar of mustard and some salt in a twist of paper and you're away. Or else, take a nice wedge of veal and ham pie, or an egg and bacon tart. Then there's your ploughman's lunch – tailor-made picnic fare. Just add Branston pickle and go. The great English roast can also be the picnic's biggest hit, left to go cold and sliced up the next day into big hearty chunks with fresh bread and pickles. With all that going for us, we should be the best picnickers in the world.

tony

I love the whole idea of barbecues – any excuse to be outside and drop the formal manners and the elbows-off-the table mentality. For me, my garden is merely an extension of my living room. At the moment, I'm building a big wood-fired oven and barbecue out there, which has got Giorgio all excited. He's promised to come over with half a baby goat or something, to show me how to get the most out of it. Personally, I think the very first meal it produces should be a nice whole Scottish salmon – although Giorgio's very welcome to cook it for me if he wants.

You can, however, get a bit carried away with the whole barbecue thing. Go down to your garden centre and you'll see people paying six, seven hundred quid for a barbecue. There seems to be an unofficial race going on in the suburbs to see who can get the biggest, brightest, most technically advanced set-up and who's got the most knobs, whistles and optional extras. It's only a barbecue, guys, not a Ferrari.

Too many people spend all their efforts on the barbecue and not on the food. The trick is not to think of your barbecue as a burger and sausage dispenser. Anything you can do on your grill inside, you can do outside on the barbecue – and more often than not it's going to taste better. Your average Brit would say, 'Oh, you can't cook Dover sole fillets on the barbecue', which is nonsense. The best Dover sole I ever tasted was at a barbecue. You get that pure sole flavour, but you also get just that tickle of smoke that really lifts it a peg or two.

Put two bits of metal over your barbecue and stick a chicken on it and you're going to have spit-roasted chicken as good as anything you could do in your fancy automatic oven rotisserie.

Of course, the real problem with the English barbecue is that we've transformed the whole experience into something out of a corny sixties American TV series. The host wears a big floppy chef's hat and a silly apron emblazoned with 'Come 'n' get it', while all the men stand at one end of the garden talking about football and all the women stand at the other end talking about the men.

Of course, when it's your barbecue you're not just the cook. Suddenly you transform into this big buck deer, answering the call of the wild, the lure of the outdoors. That's not a chef's hat on your head, that's a pair of magnificent antlers. All of which tells me, we really don't get out enough.

For a salad, my father would walk over to the vegetable garden and yank out handfuls of salad greens and a couple of tomatoes, and there was your salad.

When it comes to barbecues, my father was the acknowledged master in our village. Originally the barbecue itself had belonged to my grandfather, but my father was the one who put wheels on it, and he was for ever wheeling it out into the garden or on to the terrace. Maybe that's why I like motorbikes so much.

His routine was always the same. First, he would place ashes on the base, then cover those with bits of wood and start a big, roaring fire. Then he would let the fire subside, break it all down and get the ashes from underneath, which he spread on top. Then he'd close the flue and the whole thing would die right down. After ten minutes, he would open the flue again and it would spring back into life. It was an art and a science. He was brilliant with that barbecue. He could cook anything on it.

Unfortunately my brother, who used to help him sometimes, was not what you'd call a natural. For him, more was always better. He used to get the flames so high that the poor food never stood a chance.

But my father was a perfectionist. First he would do the bread and the vegetables, while Mum would be inside cooking pasta – baked pasta in winter and a lighter *spaghetti al crudo* in summer. Then he would cook the fish: never just one type of fish, always two – perhaps a whole sea bass and some fresh prawns. Next would come the meat. One of his favourites was *galletti* – small baby chickens cut down the backbone, flattened and then marinated with dried chilli, lemon, olive oil and his secret ingredient, Worcestershire sauce. Actually it was my secret ingredient because I'm the one who introduced him to it.

For a salad, my father would walk over to the vegetable garden and yank out handfuls of salad greens and a couple of tomatoes, and there was your salad. The wheels of that barbecue must have had a very loud squeak, because every time he rolled it out, people came from everywhere. Cousins, uncles, kids – you name it.

giorgio

131

Recipes
Alfresco

Taramasalata

Pinzimonio con le due salse

Vitello tonnato

Hummous

Torta di vegetali

Scotch eggs

Carpione di pesce

Barbecued salmon with cucumber and dill

Barbecued pork belly with Chinese cabbage

Chicken liver parfait

Seafood skewers with rice salad

Caponata di melanzane

Pickled onions and gherkins with tarragon

Smoked haddock and ricotta tart

Acciughe marinate

Focaccia con cipolle rosse

Insalata di carciofi alla Parmigiana

Peaches in red wine

Taramasalata

Taramasalata

In England, we generally throw away the cod's roe and keep just the flesh, which must give the Greeks, who turn the roe into taramasalata, a bit of a chuckle. I love the taste of the smoked roe – it has what I call an ancient flavour. **Tony**

Serves 4

50g/2oz fresh white breadcrumbs
200g/7oz smoked cod's roe,
    skinned and diced
200ml/7fl oz olive oil
juice of 1–2 lemons

4–5 tablespoons water
handful of kalamata olives
1 tablespoon extra virgin olive oil
pitta bread, to serve

Place the breadcrumbs and cod's roe in a food processor and pulse until roughly blended. With the motor running, gradually pour in the olive oil. Now add the lemon juice and water a little at a time, checking for flavour and consistency – you may not need it all. Spoon the taramasalata into a serving bowl, cover and chill until ready to serve. Scatter with the olives, drizzle the extra virgin olive oil on top and serve with pitta bread, lightly warmed in the oven.

Pinzimonio con le due salse
Crudités with two sauces

Pinzimonio was originally a way of eating raw vegetables, dipping them into a rustic 'sauce' of olive oil, salt and pepper. The dish has now travelled all over Italy, with a variety of sauces that change from region to region. Here are two of my favourites, one rocket and the other lemon. **Giorgio**

Serves 6

4 celery stalks
4 carrots
1 cucumber
2 fennel bulbs
small bunch of radishes
5 spring onions
2 chicory heads
sea salt and freshly ground black
    pepper

For the rocket sauce:
2 handfuls of rocket leaves
50ml/2fl oz olive oil

For the lemon sauce:
juice of 2 lemons
100ml/3½fl oz olive oil

Peel the celery, carrots and cucumber and cut them into sticks about 5cm/2in long. Remove the tough outer layer from the fennel bulbs and cut the fennel into quarters. Trim the radishes and spring onions and separate the chicory into leaves. Put all the vegetables in a bowl, cover and leave in the fridge.

For the rocket sauce, whiz the rocket in a food processor with the olive oil. Season with salt and transfer to a bowl.

For the lemon sauce, put the lemon juice in a bowl with a pinch of salt and pepper and slowly whisk in the olive oil.

Arrange all the vegetables on a large platter and serve with the sauces in 2 small bowls on the side.

Vitello tonnato

Veal with tuna sauce

Vitello is veal and *tonnato* is a creamy tuna sauce. Together, they make a wonderful dish to eat outdoors. If you're picnicking, do what my grandmother did and layer the sliced veal and sauce in a plastic container. It was messy to eat, but nobody seemed to worry about that. If you're dining al fresco closer to home, arrange the veal on a large platter and coat with the sauce. Not as messy, but just as good. **Giorgio**

Serves 6

1kg/2¼lb eye round fillet of veal
1 carrot, roughly chopped
1 onion, roughly chopped
2 bay leaves
3 cloves
3 juniper berries
1 bottle of dry white wine

For the sauce:
2 egg yolks
300ml/½ pint light olive oil
50ml/2fl oz white wine vinegar
juice of 1 lemon
200g/7oz canned tuna in oil, drained
handful of capers, rinsed and
     drained, plus a few to garnish
sea salt

Place the veal in a non-metallic bowl with the carrot, onion, bay leaves, cloves and juniper berries and cover with the white wine. Cover and leave to marinate in the fridge overnight.

The next day, take the veal out of the marinade, wrap it tightly in a piece of muslin or a tea towel to form a sausage shape, and tie with string. Place the veal in a large pan and pour in the marinade. Bring gently to a simmer, then cover and cook for 35–40 minutes, until tender. Remove from the heat and leave the veal to cool completely in the liquid.

Meanwhile, make the sauce. In a bowl, whisk the egg yolks and 2 pinches of salt together. Add the olive oil a drop at a time, whisking energetically, to make a mayonnaise; you can start to add the oil in a thin stream once a third of it has been incorporated. Add enough of the vinegar and lemon juice to give a pouring consistency. Put the tuna and capers in a food processor and whiz to a purée, then stir into the mayonnaise.

Unwrap the cooled veal and cut it into slices about 5mm/¼in thick. Arrange the slices on a large serving platter and spoon the tuna sauce over the top. Garnish with a few capers before serving.

Hummous

Hummous

Dips are made for picnics, and home-made dips taste so much better and fresher than bought ones. You can scoop anything you like through them – raw vegetables, Scandinavian crisp-breads, Greek pitta bread or crusty French bread. **Tony**

Serves 4

2 small garlic cloves, roughly chopped

1 mild red chilli, deseeded and roughly chopped

400g/14oz can of chickpeas, drained and rinsed

4 tablespoons extra virgin olive oil

handful of parsley or coriander leaves, roughly chopped

juice of ½ lemon

sea salt and freshly ground black pepper

Put the garlic and chilli in a food processor and whiz until finely chopped. Add the chickpeas and a tablespoon or two of the olive oil and whiz until completely smooth – this may take several minutes. Add the herbs and a squeeze of lemon juice and whiz again until well blended. Taste and add more lemon juice and olive oil, as needed, plus some salt and pepper.

Spoon into a serving bowl, drizzle over a little more oil, then cover and chill until ready to serve.

Torta di vegetali
Vegetable tart

This is Italy's answer to the French *tarte aux blettes*, although we prefer to throw in some rice and courgettes along with the spinach and Swiss chard to give it a little more substance. This is the easiest way to eat up your vegetables on a picnic. **Giorgio**

Serves 4

150g/5oz spinach
1–2 large Swiss chard stalks,
    weighing about 200g/7oz
300g/10oz courgettes, thinly sliced
1 onion, thinly sliced
100g/4oz arborio or carnaroli rice
50g/2oz Parmesan cheese, freshly
    grated
2 eggs, beaten
sea salt and freshly ground black
    pepper

For the pastry:
300g/10oz plain flour
pinch of salt
150ml/$\frac{1}{4}$ pint water
1 teaspoon olive oil
1 egg
2 tablespoons milk

To make the pastry, put the flour and salt in a bowl, then stir in the water and oil to make a smooth, firm dough. Cover with a damp cloth and leave to rest for at least 10 minutes.

Preheat the oven to 180°C/350°F/Gas Mark 4. Plunge the spinach into a large pan of boiling water for a few seconds until it wilts, then drain well and set aside. Cut the green leafy part off the chard. Cook the stalks in a large pan of boiling water for 2 minutes, then add the leafy part and cook for a further 30 seconds. Drain well, then cut the stalks into strips 1cm/$\frac{1}{2}$in wide. Mix together the spinach, chard, courgettes, onion, rice, Parmesan, eggs and some salt and pepper and set aside.

Halve the pastry and roll out each piece until it is 5mm/$\frac{1}{4}$in thick. Use one half to line an oiled 18cm/7in pie dish or tart tin. Spoon in the filling, then cover with the remaining half of pastry. Trim the edges and press well together to seal. Beat together the egg and milk and brush over the pie and sprinkle with sea salt. Bake for 50 minutes, until golden brown. Serve hot, warm or cold.

Scotch eggs
Uova Scozzesi

They say an egg is the world's best packaging. Well, here's a perfect package inside a perfect package. Everyone loves Scotch eggs. Not to love them would be almost un-British. That said, if you can find those amazingly crisp Japanese 'panko' breadcrumbs in an Oriental store or food hall, they're even better. **Tony**

Serves 4

4 eggs
350g/12oz fine sausagemeat
4 tablespoons chopped parsley
2 anchovy fillets in oil, drained
    and finely chopped
2 tablespoons capers, rinsed,
    drained and finely chopped
50g/2oz smoked ham, finely
    chopped

vegetable oil for deep-frying
sea salt and freshly ground black
    pepper

For the coating:
1 egg, beaten
6 tablespoons natural golden dried
    breadcrumbs

Bring a pan of water to a simmer and add the eggs. Simmer for 8 minutes, then drain, rinse in cold water and shell.

Mix the sausagemeat with the parsley, anchovies, capers and ham and season well with salt and pepper. Divide the mixture into quarters. Shape each piece into a flat cake and mould around a boiled egg as evenly as possible. Brush with the beaten egg and roll in the breadcrumbs until thoroughly coated. Chill, uncovered, for 3–4 hours, or overnight.

Heat the oil in a deep-fat fryer or a large, deep saucepan until it is hot enough to brown a cube of bread in 1 minute. Gently lower each egg into the oil and deep-fry for 7–8 minutes, until golden brown. Remove and drain on kitchen paper. Serve hot or cold.

Carpione di pesce
Marinated sardines

This is a speciality of my native Lombardy. The technique of frying the fish before marinating it in oil, vinegar and wine works particularly well with freshwater fish and oily fish like sardines. Don't ask me why, but they always seem to taste so much better when eaten outdoors. **Giorgio**

Serves 4

vegetable oil for deep-frying
8 sardines, scaled, cleaned and filleted
2 tablespoons plain flour
400ml/14fl oz olive oil
2 garlic cloves, peeled
3 bay leaves
1 sprig of parsley
2 sprigs of rosemary

4 juniper berries
3 black peppercorns
4 cloves
150ml/$\frac{1}{4}$ pint white wine vinegar
75ml/2$\frac{1}{2}$fl oz white wine
2 onions, finely sliced
sea salt and freshly ground black pepper

Heat the vegetable oil in a deep-fat fryer or a large, deep saucepan until it is hot enough to brown a cube of bread in 1 minute. Dust the sardine fillets with the flour, shaking off any excess, then drop them into the hot oil and fry for 2 minutes. Remove with a slotted spoon and drain on kitchen paper. Arrange the sardines in a single layer in a large, shallow dish.

Heat the olive oil in a saucepan and add the garlic, herbs, juniper berries, peppercorns and cloves. When the garlic and herbs start to fry, remove from the heat and leave to cool for 10 minutes. Slowly add the white wine vinegar, then return to the heat. Once all the water from the vinegar has evaporated, increase the temperature a little and repeat the process with the white wine. Add the onions and let the mixture come slowly to a simmer. Cook gently for 10–15 minutes, then set aside to infuse for 1 hour. Pour the warm marinade over the sardines, cover and leave to marinate overnight.

Barbecued salmon with cucumber and dill

Salmone al griglia con cetriolo e aneto

We tend to overcook salmon in this country, so here I've treated it in much the same way as the Japanese do their *tataki* of tuna – lightly searing the outside ahead of time and leaving the inside pink and glistening. The marinade gives it a silky, vaguely gravad lax feel. **Tony**

Serves 4

4 pieces of salmon fillet, about 11cm/4½in thick (taken from the thick side of the salmon and not the belly), skinned

For the marinade:
300ml/½ pint white wine
large bunch of dill, roughly chopped, plus extra to garnish
4 tablespoons olive oil
3 tablespoons cognac

12 peppercorns, lightly crushed
3 tablespoons rock salt
3 tablespoons sugar

For the cucumber salad:
1 cucumber
150g/5oz plain yoghurt
juice of ½ lemon
4 tablespoons chopped dill
sea salt and freshly ground black pepper

Place the pieces of salmon in a shallow dish in a single layer. Mix together all the marinade ingredients and pour over the salmon. Cover with clingfilm and leave in the fridge overnight.

To make the salad, peel the cucumber and cut it in half lengthways. Scoop out and discard the seeds and finely slice the cucumber. Put it in a bowl with the yoghurt, lemon juice and dill and toss together well, seasoning to taste.

Remove the salmon from the marinade, drain well and cook over medium coals on the barbecue for no more than 45 seconds on each side – just enough to sear the outside of the fish. Leave to cool, then place in the fridge for 1 hour.

Cut the salmon into slices 5mm/¼in thick and arrange on a serving plate. Garnish with a little extra dill and serve with the cucumber salad.

Barbecued pork belly with Chinese cabbage

Pancetta alla griglia con cavolo Cinese

There's a whole United Nations of flavours in this. Don't let the amount of work or cooking time put you off. It's worth it. **Tony**

Serves 4

1.3kg/3lb piece of pork belly, boned
2 carrots, roughly chopped
1 large onion, roughly chopped
2 pinches of Chinese five-spice
    powder
1 star anise
1 bay leaf
a few black peppercorns
1 jar (about 300g/10oz) of Creole or
    Cajun barbecue sauce or
    cooking sauce

For the Chinese cabbage:
2 tablespoons olive oil
1 garlic clove, finely chopped
$1/2$–1 red chilli, deseeded and finely
    chopped

1 tablespoon finely chopped fresh
    root ginger
2 carrots, cut into long ribbons
2 heads of pak choy, leaves
    separated
1 head of Chinese cabbage, roughly
    chopped
1 bunch of spring onions, sliced on
    the diagonal into 1cm/$1/2$in
    lengths
2 teaspoons Worcestershire sauce
4 tablespoons chicken stock
1 teaspoon sesame oil
sea salt and freshly ground black
    pepper

Remove the skin and most of the fat from the pork, then put the meat in a large saucepan with the bones, if you have them. Cover with plenty of cold water and bring to the boil. Drain well, then return to the pan and cover with fresh water. Add all the remaining ingredients except the sauce and bring slowly to the boil. Skim off the scum from the surface and simmer very gently for about 2 hours, until the pork feels very tender when you push a skewer through it. Leave to cool in its liquid, then remove and drain well. Place the pork in a baking tin, put another baking tin on top and weight down. Leave in the fridge overnight.

    The next day, cut the pork into 4, removing excess fat if necessary, and place it in a shallow baking dish. Pour over the sauce, turning the meat to coat it in the sauce, then cover and leave in the fridge for 6–8 hours or overnight.

    Bring the pork to room temperature and cook on a barbecue or in an oven preheated to 220°C/425°F/Gas Mark 7 for 20–30 minutes, until well browned.

    Meanwhile, prepare the Chinese cabbage. Heat the olive oil in a wok or large frying pan, add the garlic, chilli and ginger and stir-fry for 1–2 minutes, until aromatic. Add the carrots and stir-fry for 1 minute, then toss in the pak choy and Chinese cabbage and stir-fry for 1–2 minutes. Add the spring onions and cook for 1 minute longer, then add the Worcestershire sauce, followed by the chicken stock. Cover the pan and simmer for 1 minute. Stir in the sesame oil, toss everything together well and adjust the seasoning if necessary.

Divide the Chinese cabbage between 4 serving plates. Slice each piece of pork, arrange on top of the cabbage and serve immediately.

Chicken liver parfait

Terrina di fegato di pollo

This is better known as a fancy restaurant starter than a picnic dish, but for me its flavour always improves with the addition of some crusty bread and plenty of fresh air. I love the way that something as mundane as chicken livers can be transformed into such a rich, creamy and elegant dish. **Tony**

Serves 6–8

75ml/2½fl oz white wine
2 shallots, finely chopped
75ml/2½fl oz port
75ml/2½fl oz Madeira
250g/9oz chicken livers
2 garlic cloves, finely chopped

1 egg
1 egg yolk
200g/7oz unsalted butter, melted
1 sprig of rosemary, chopped
sea salt and freshly ground black
  pepper

Preheat the oven to 180°C/350°F/Gas Mark 4. Put the white wine and shallots in a saucepan and simmer gently for about 10 minutes, until the wine has reduced by half. At the same time simmer the port and Madeira in another saucepan until it has reduced by half. Add the port and Madeira to the reduced wine and shallot mixture and leave to cool.

Rinse and drain the chicken livers, then put them in a food processor with the shallot, port and Madeira mixture and process until smooth. Add the garlic and plenty of salt and pepper and process until smooth again. Add the egg and egg yolk and process for 30 seconds, then pour in the melted butter and process until the mixture is creamy.

Line a 450g/1lb loaf tin with buttered foil and pour in the mixture. Sprinkle the chopped rosemary over the top and place the loaf tin in a roasting tin. Pour enough hot water into the roasting tin to come half-way up the sides of the loaf tin, then place in the oven and cook for 50 minutes, until firm when pressed gently with a finger. Leave to cool completely and then chill. Turn out of the tin and cut into slices to serve.

Seafood skewers with rice salad

Spiedini di pesce con insalata di riso

A barbecue isn't a barbecue without a rice salad, but that doesn't mean it has to be boring and predictable. The samphire and asparagus in this one make a great accompaniment to the seafood, and the dressing also acts as a dressing for the skewers. **Tony**

Serves 4

1 monkfish tail, cut into bite-sized
    cubes
12 large peeled raw prawns
8 large scallops
25g/1oz unsalted butter, melted
sea salt and freshly ground black
    pepper

For the rice salad:
12oz/350g long grain rice
100g/3¹/₂oz sprue (thin) asparagus
150g/5oz fresh samphire

For the dressing:
45ml/1¹/₂fl oz white wine vinegar
125ml/4fl oz olive oil
1 tablespoon water
6 cornichons (baby gherkins), finely
    chopped
4 tablespoons capers, drained,
    rinsed and finely chopped
large bunch of flat-leaf parsley,
    finely chopped
large bunch of chervil, roughly
    chopped

For the salad, cook the rice in plenty of boiling water for 10 minutes, until tender. Drain well and place in a large serving dish.

Bring a large saucepan of water to the boil, plunge in the asparagus and cook for no more than 30 seconds. Add the samphire and cook for a minute longer, then drain in a colander and run under cold water to refresh. Pat dry with kitchen paper and gently toss into the rice. Mix all the ingredients for the dressing together and pour it over the rice, stirring to coat well.

Thread the monkfish cubes, prawns and scallops on to 4 skewers and brush with the melted butter. Season lightly with a little sea salt and plenty of pepper. Place the fish skewers over medium-hot coals on the barbecue (or on a hot griddle if you are cooking indoors) and cook for about 3–4 minutes, turning regularly to char the fish all over. Serve hot, with the rice salad.

Caponata di melanzane
Sweet and sour aubergine

When an Italian dish contains aubergines, pine nuts and sultanas, it's a good bet that it comes from Sicily. Caponata is a cross between a relish and a cooked vegetable salad, and makes perfect picnic food. At home, it also works well as an accompaniment to fish or poultry. **Giorgio**

1 large aubergine, cut into
    2cm/^{3}/$_4$in cubes
1 tablespoon olive oil
1 onion, cut into 1cm/^{1}/$_2$in dice
vegetable oil for deep–frying
2 celery stalks, cut into 1cm/^{1}/$_2$in
    dice
^{1}/$_2$ fennel bulb, cut into 1cm/^{1}/$_2$in
    dice
about 125ml/4fl oz extra virgin
    olive oil

75ml/2^1/$_2$fl oz good-quality red wine
    vinegar
50g/2oz sultanas
50g/2oz pine nuts
3 plum tomatoes, cut into 2cm/^{3}/$_4$in
    dice
bunch of basil, chopped
2 teaspoons caster sugar
sea salt and freshly ground black
    pepper

Put the aubergine in a colander, sprinkle liberally with salt and leave to drain for at least 2 hours. Meanwhile, heat the olive oil in a frying pan, add the onion and sauté until soft. Transfer to a large bowl.

Rinse the aubergine and drain thoroughly. Heat the vegetable oil in a deep-fat fryer or a large, deep saucepan until it is hot enough to brown a cube of bread in 1 minute. Add the celery and fry for 1–2 minutes, until tender and golden. Remove with a slotted spoon and drain on kitchen paper. Repeat with the fennel and aubergine.

Add the deep-fried vegetables to the onion. Season with salt and then add the extra virgin olive oil, red wine vinegar and salt and pepper to taste. Stir in the sultanas, pine nuts, tomatoes, basil and sugar. Cover and leave to infuse for at least 2 hours.

Pickled onions and gherkins with tarragon

Cipolle conservate e cetriolini al dragoncello

I inherited my love of pickled onions from my Dad. I don't know whether he'd approve of me mucking about with them like this, but then again, they're still pickled onions, aren't they? The two tricks here are the salting overnight to get all the moisture out, and the addition of tarragon, which gives such a nice, aromatic, aniseedy character. **Tony**

1.3kg/3lb fresh gherkins or baby
   cucumbers
250g/9oz rock salt
1.3kg/3lb pickling onions, peeled
8 garlic cloves, peeled and halved
large bunch of tarragon
6 small red chillies

12 mixed peppercorns
1.3 litres/2¼ pints white wine
   vinegar, plus extra for topping
   up the jars
1.3 litres/2¼ pints pickling vinegar
   or malt vinegar

Wash the gherkins and then rub them in a towel to remove the tiny spikes and to dry completely. Lay them in a shallow tray in a single layer and completely cover with the rock salt. Leave overnight.

Sterilise two 2 litre/3½ pint Kilner jars by washing them in hot soapy water, rinsing well and then drying in a very low oven for 30 minutes.

Shake the salt from the gherkins and place a few of them in a single layer in the jars. Top with the pickling onions, then with a couple of garlic halves, a few tarragon leaves, a whole chilli and a few peppercorns. Continue layering in this manner until all the ingredients are used up.

Bring the white wine vinegar and pickling vinegar to the boil, pour them over the gherkins and onions and leave to cool. The onions and gherkins will absorb the vinegar, so keep topping the jars up with extra vinegar over the next 2 days. Seal and store in a cool, dry place for 2 months before use.

Smoked haddock and ricotta tart

Torta di aglefino affumicato e ricotta

This is one of the truly great pairings of the food world. The light, almost anonymous taste of the ricotta trades off perfectly with the dense, sturdy flavour of the smoked haddock. You can almost imagine something like this being eaten in medieval times. **Tony**

Serves 4

1 quantity of Tony's shortcrust pastry (see page 245)
125g/4oz smoked haddock fillet
200ml/7fl oz milk
250g/9oz fresh spinach
3 eggs
250g/9oz ricotta cheese
250ml/9fl oz double cream

50g/2oz Parmesan cheese, freshly grated
pinch of cayenne pepper
1 garlic clove, finely chopped (optional)
sea salt and freshly ground black pepper

Preheat the oven to 190°C/375°F/Gas Mark 5. Roll out the pastry and use to line a 20cm/8in loose-bottomed tart tin. Line with greaseproof paper, fill with baking beans and bake for 15 minutes, until lightly golden. Remove the baking beans and paper and set aside.

Place the smoked haddock in a pan and pour over the milk. Bring to the boil and simmer for 3–4 minutes, until the fish is just cooked. Drain, discarding the milk, and set aside.

Wash the spinach and place in a pan with just the water clinging to its leaves. Cook over a gentle heat for 2–3 minutes, until just wilted. Drain the spinach and, using your hands, squeeze out any excess water. Roughly chop the spinach and set aside.

In a large bowl, mix together the eggs, ricotta, double cream, Parmesan, cayenne pepper and garlic, if using. Season with salt and pepper. Roughly flake the fish and gently fold it into the egg and ricotta mixture with the chopped spinach. Spoon the mixture into the pastry case and bake for 20–25 minutes, until golden and just firm to the touch.

Acciughe marinate
Marinated anchovies

Don't even think about canned anchovies – these are nothing like them. My idea of the perfect start to a summer lunch is to be sitting outdoors with the sun on my back, a glass of chilled white wine in hand and a plate of marinated anchovies in front of me. **Giorgio**

Serves 4

**10 very fresh anchovies, scaled and
cleaned
250ml/8fl oz olive oil
2 large red chillies, finely chopped
2 garlic cloves, cut into quarters**

**1 bay leaf
1 sprig of rosemary
juice of 2 lemons
50ml/2fl oz white wine vinegar**

Using a sharp filleting knife, make a small incision just below the head of each anchovy, through the flesh to the bone. Cut off the fins and carefully cut along the backbone to the tail. Lift off the fillet and repeat on the other side. Remove the pinbones from the fillet and pat dry with kitchen paper.

In a bowl, mix together the olive oil, chillies, garlic, bay leaf, rosemary, lemon juice and vinegar and leave to infuse for 10 minutes. Lay the anchovies in a large shallow dish and slowly spoon the marinade over the top. Cover and leave to marinate overnight before serving.

Focaccia con cipolle rosse

Red onion focaccia

There's nothing quite like the smell of fresh, home-baked focaccia as it comes out of the oven. In our house, if it can make it from the oven to the kitchen table in one piece it is considered something of a triumph. This recipe, which is very simple and user-friendly, is almost a cross between focaccia and ciabatta. While Easyblend yeast is usually added directly to the flour, I find mixing it with the water first makes it easier to handle here. **Giorgio**

Serves 8–10

700ml/24fl oz warm water
3 x 7g sachets of Easyblend yeast,
    or 25g/1oz fresh yeast
1kg/2$\frac{1}{4}$lb Italian 'OO' flour

20g/^{3}/$_4$oz salt
200ml/7fl oz olive oil
1 red onion

Pour the water into a large bowl and either sprinkle over the dried yeast or crumble in the fresh yeast. Whisk together until frothy and combined. Add the flour and salt to the water and mix together with your hands until you have a soft, sticky dough; be very careful not to over-work the mixture. Pour over 5 tablespoons of the olive oil, cover with a tea-towel and leave in a warm place for about 30 minutes, until the dough has at least doubled in size.

    Drizzle 2 tablespoons of the olive oil on to a work surface and tip the dough out on to it. Keep carefully turning the dough over in the oil for about 1 minute, gently stretching it but again being careful not to overwork it. Return to the bowl and drizzle over another 2 table-spoons of oil. Cover with a tea-towel and leave to rise in a warm place again for 30 minutes. Meanwhile, preheat the oven to its highest setting

    Peel the red onion and slice it very finely, preferably using a mandoline. Oil a large baking tin, about 30 x 40cm/12 x 16in, or 2 smaller baking tins. Tip the dough into the tin and press it out to fit. Press all over the top with your fingertips to leave indents. Scatter the red onion over the top, drizzle with the remaining oil and bake for 20–30 minutes, until risen and golden. Leave to cool, then cut into squares to serve.

Insalata di carciofi alla Parmigiana

Artichoke and Parmesan salad

I'm crazy about that lovely tannic flavour of artichokes. They really are the perfect picnic food, either served as part of an antipasto platter or just served up with a few slices of salami or prosciutto. While there's nothing wrong with the preserved artichokes you buy in jars, nothing comes close to fresh artichokes that you have prepared yourself. You'll know what I mean when you taste this marvellous salad. **Giorgio**

Serves 4

**4 globe artichokes
2 lemons, cut in half
2 chicory heads
100ml/3½fl oz Giorgio's vinaigrette
(see page 243)
4 handfuls of mixed salad leaves
4 tablespoons freshly grated
Parmesan cheese, plus a few
shavings of Parmesan to garnish
about 12 chive stalks, cut into long
pieces
sea salt and freshly ground black
pepper**

**For the marinade:
200ml/7fl oz extra virgin olive oil
1 garlic clove, peeled
1 bay leaf
1 sprig of rosemary
1 sprig of thyme
2 peppercorns
4 tablespoons red wine vinegar
(one of the less-acidic
varieties)**

Slice about a third off the top of each artichoke. Snap off the stalks, then pull off the leaves, leaving only the pale, tender inner ones. With a small sharp knife, trim the base of each artichoke until you expose the tender heart. Rub with one of the lemon halves and place in a bowl of water acidulated with some of the lemon juice. When you have prepared all the artichokes, put them in a large pan of boiling water, add the lemon halves, squeezing in any juice that is left, and cover with a plate to submerge them in the water. Simmer for 15–20 minutes, until the artichokes are just tender when pierced with a knife. Leave to cool in their cooking liquid, then drain well, cut into quarters and scrape out the choke with a teaspoon. Place in a bowl.

Put all the ingredients for the marinade except the red wine vinegar in a small saucepan and bring slowly to the boil. When the garlic begins to brown, remove from the heat and pour in the vinegar a little at a time. Pour the marinade over the artichokes and leave overnight.

Separate the chicory leaves, toss them with a little of the vinaigrette and season to taste. Arrange them around the edge of 4 large serving plates, with the tips pointing outwards. Place the marinated artichokes on top. Toss the salad leaves with the remaining vinaigrette,

Peaches in red wine

Pesche al vino rosso

Rarely has so little work been rewarded with so much flavour. I pinched this one from Giorgio, who would naturally and inevitably use an Italian red wine, but I find it works just as well with a good Pinot Noir or a New World Merlot. **Tony**

Serves 6

1 bottle of good fruity red wine   **6 large, slightly underripe peaches**
50g/2oz caster sugar

Halve the peaches, remove the stones and slice thinly. Place in a large bowl, sprinkle with the sugar and pour over the wine. Leave overnight in the fridge, then bring to room temperature for 2 hours before serving. Eat on a warm, sunny day, ladled into wine glasses.

Kids

Good adults' food is also good children's food. **Giorgio**

giorgio

I get really mad when we go to a restaurant that has a special children's menu. First of all, these special menus are usually full of stupid processed things you wouldn't dream of eating yourself. Secondly, if it's a good restaurant it will already have plenty of things that will be perfectly all right for kids anyway. Good adults' food is also good children's food.

I hate the idea of putting children at a special table by themselves away from the grown-ups, too. The conviviality of the table is one of the most important things you can teach children. How are they going to learn that when you're on one table and they have been relegated to another?

In Italy, the dinner table isn't just somewhere to eat, it is somewhere to socialise, to communicate and to share. One of the biggest crimes you can commit is not to be at the table in time for dinner. It is an unwritten law that the pasta doesn't go into the water until the last person is seated, because overcooked pasta is even more of a disaster than being late for dinner. So if you're not there in time, your entire family sits there starving. And when you do turn up, they make sure you know that it's your fault. It's a good lesson.

The most important stage in feeding most children is the first two forkfuls. At the start of a meal they'd rather be playing, or doing anything but eating. But get past the first two forkfuls and you're over the biggest hurdle, because they can then think about what they've just tasted, and hopefully they'll eat the lot.

Sometimes you have to play with food a little to make it to their liking. Not that we want to create a nation of fish finger-eaters, but because kids are drawn to recognisable shapes. For example, when we do steak, Margherita's meat comes off the grill first before everyone else's so it's really rare, then we cut it into pieces and sauté all the pieces lightly on all sides. She loves it, but she wouldn't touch it if we gave her one big slab of meat.

The best way to feed children is to treat them as equals, although there are sometimes special circumstances. Margherita, for instance, has some pretty serious allergies, which means she can't eat many things we would all normally eat, such as seafood, eggs, tomatoes, bread, strawberries, and quite a lot of other stuff as well.

It's a challenge, but there are always ways around it. We now have forty-five tried-and-tested recipes for lentils, which Margherita loves. Plaxy has even perfected a lentil shepherd's pie, which has become a family favourite. Jack, on the other hand, is a pushover. He'll eat absolutely anything.

tony

What we all have to do is get children used to good food early on, and by that I don't mean keep banging on about how they have to eat their greens or they won't get any dessert, or any of that sort of nonsense. We have to somehow make them think that the greens and all the rest are the good part. So the real threat should be: if you don't eat up your dessert you won't get any greens next time.

Part of the answer here is to get kids involved in the cooking process as early as you can. Make them feel clever and talented for being able to make a pasta dish or whatever and that dish is going to taste as good as any Big Mac. Make the good stuff seem fun and the fun stuff won't look quite as tantalising.

If you have a fussy eater, it can be more about getting attention than any real dislike of the food involved. Most of us will give in if a child refuses to eat anything but one special food, because, we reason, at least they're eating something. There is no easy answer, but try not to make a big issue of it. Perhaps don't say anything at all for a while and give the pressure a chance to ease off. Or try serving the family meal in the middle of the table and letting everyone help themselves to their own food, which teaches them a sense of individual responsibility. Kids are pretty smart, you know. They'll try to get around meal times, but you can't just let them snack whenever they want and you can't let them manipulate you, or you'll be setting up some really bad patterns for the future. Very young children, of course, need smaller amounts of food more often, but once they get older you have to get tougher. If you don't feed them between meals, they'll soon learn to eat what is in front of them, without it being a parent/child issue.

I do think that the sort of food you're brought up with plays a big part in shaping your character. I divide kids into two camps. There are the ones who go for brown sauce and the ones who prefer tomato ketchup. Adventurous kids who try anything are brown sauce kids; kids who have no food curiosity go for the ketchup. All kids go through a tomato ketchup phase and that's okay. But you also want them to move on, like my kids, and be hungry for other experiences as well.

I don't think we can get too high and mighty about the food our kids eat. I think the ideal parents lie somewhere in the middle, between Mr and Mrs Organic Food Aware and Mr and Mrs Lazy, who just send their children off to the nearest burger chain.

Obviously children should eat fish – it's rich in protein and B vitamins, and the omega-3 fatty acids in salmon, mackerel, herring, sardines and tuna are really beneficial – but rather than try to force it down their necks and bludgeon them into eating it, I think we should compete with the fast-food chains on their own ground. If I give our children a nice fillet of haddock or halibut in a really light batter with home-made chips and all the trimmings, they'll eat it.

At our fish! restaurants we've developed some excellent alternatives to fast food, designed to appeal to our younger diners. Rather than churning out a mass-produced burger of anonymous meat and dubious flavour, we make a burger out of chopped fresh tuna. They get the whole burger experience, they get lots of flavour, and they get something that's doing them good.

When you reach the stage where your kids can walk past the fast-food shop and say, my Mum does it better, then you're really making progress.

tony

...we make a burger out of chopped fresh tuna. They get the whole burger experience, they get lots of flavour, and they get something that's doing them good.

v. fast food

What you have to remember is that most fast food started life as something pretty respectable, so if they want fast food, give them the real thing.

Basically, there is nothing at all wrong with a hamburger. If you buy some really good minced beef, nice gherkins and fresh salad onions, add some home-made mayonnaise, a bit of French or American mustard or ketchup, and put it all into a proper bun, the kids won't want to go back to the burger shop because they'll know they can do better at home.

The other day, my son Jack went off with a school friend to buy a computer game. Afterwards he still had five pounds left over, but instead of blowing it on burgers, he came home and made toasted cheese sandwiches in the sandwich maker we brought back from America.

When I got home, there he was like some great television chef, showing his mate how to make a toasted sandwich. 'You have to spread the butter on the outside of the bread, then take your cheese and place it on top,' he was saying. He was very good. He should have his own show!

giorgio

Recipes
Kids

Scaloppine al formaggio

Home-made tomato soup

Minestrone

Monkfish nuggets

Lasagne al ragu di carne

Easy spaghetti bolognese

Chicken schnitzel

Giorgio's pizza

Fish pie

Petto di pollo al marsala

Tuna burger

Salsicce con polenta

Insalata verde con Parmigiano

Sausage and pea risotto

Torta di cioccalata alla Margherita

Locobocker glory

Scaloppine al formaggio

Pork escalope with melted cheese

My kids love *scaloppine* because it is cut so thin and doesn't overwhelm them with a great, scary slab of meat. They particularly like this one because of the cheese. Put melted cheese on anything and I guarantee you, kids will eat it. **Giorgio**

Serves 4

600g/1lb 5oz pork fillet
2 tablespoons plain flour
3 eggs
pinch of salt

100g/3½oz breadcrumbs
100ml/3½fl oz sunflower oil
100g/3½oz fontina cheese, finely
    sliced

Cut the pork fillet into 4 steaks. Flatten each steak with a meat mallet or a wooden rolling pin to about 5mm/¼in thick to make escalopes. Dust the escalopes with the flour, shaking off any excess.

Whisk the eggs in a shallow dish and add the salt. Coat the escalopes in the egg and then in the breadcrumbs, making sure they are completely covered. Heat the oil in a large frying pan, add the escalopes and fry for 2–3 minutes, until golden underneath. Turn over and place the fontina cheese on top. Cook for a further 2–3 minutes, until the other side is golden and the cheese is beginning to melt.

Home-made tomato soup

Zuppa di pomodoro casalinga

I've made it my mission with this recipe to get as close to Heinz tomato soup as I can, which keeps the kids happy. On the other hand, this has a lovely home-made freshness and a depth of flavour you'll never get out of a can, and that keeps me happy. **Tony**

Serves 4

25g/1oz unsalted butter
2 streaky bacon rashers,
    finely chopped
1 onion, finely chopped
2 sprigs of thyme
6 sprigs of flat-leaf parsley,
    roughly chopped
1 carrot, finely chopped
2 celery stalks, finely chopped

1 tablespoon tomato purée
1 tablespoon plain flour
400ml/14fl oz tomato passata
450g/1lb tomatoes, skinned,
    deseeded and chopped
400ml/14fl oz vegetable stock
150ml/¼ pint double cream
sea salt and freshly ground black
    pepper

Heat the butter in a large saucepan, add the bacon and cook for a few minutes, until it is starting to turn golden. Add the onion, thyme, parsley, carrot and celery and cook gently for 8–10 minutes, until softened but not coloured. Stir in the tomato purée and flour and mix in well. Then add the passata, chopped tomatoes and stock and simmer gently for 1 hour, until thickened and pulpy. Season with salt and pepper to taste.

Purée in a blender until smooth (strain through a sieve as well if you want a very fine consistency) and return to the saucepan. Add the double cream, check the seasoning and reheat gently.

Minestrone

Vegetable soup with pasta

To call a minestrone a vegetable soup just doesn't do it justice. This is a delicious soup, made even more kid-friendly by adding pasta, which has two things going for it. Firstly it absorbs the lovely vegetable flavours, and secondly it acts as a thickener. **Giorgio**

Serves 4

2 onions, peeled
2 carrots, peeled
1 courgette
1 celery stalk
2 potatoes, peeled
1 tomato
50g/2oz green beans
1 small cauliflower
1 small head of broccoli

1 Swiss chard stalk
2 tablespoons olive oil
3–4 garlic cloves, crushed
100g/3$\frac{1}{2}$oz peas
3 handfuls of alphabet pasta shapes
handful of spinach leaves
sea salt and freshly ground black pepper
freshly grated Parmesan cheese, to serve

Cut the onions, carrots, courgette, celery, potatoes and tomato into 1cm/$\frac{1}{2}$in dice. Top and tail the green beans and cut them into 1cm/$\frac{1}{2}$in lengths. Cut the cauliflower and broccoli into small florets. Separate the green leaf from the stalk of the Swiss chard and set aside. Cut the stalk into 1cm/$\frac{1}{2}$in dice.

Heat the olive oil in a large, deep saucepan, add the onions, carrots and garlic and sweat gently for 2–3 minutes. Then add the courgette, celery, potatoes, green beans and Swiss chard stalk and sweat until the vegetables start to yield a little moisture.

Put half the peas in a bowl and crush with the back of a fork. Add to the pan with the whole peas and cook for 3–4 minutes. Cover the vegetables with double the volume of water, bring to the boil and simmer for 10–15 minutes. Add the pasta, cook for 10 minutes, then add the broccoli and cauliflower and cook for 5 minutes. Roughly chop the spinach and the Swiss chard leaf and add to the pan. Cook for 5 minutes longer, then add the tomato and warm through for a minute or two. Season to taste and serve with grated Parmesan.

Monkfish nuggets

Bocconcini di coda di rospo

Kids love nuggets, so why not exploit this to make sure they get the goodness of white fish? As far as I'm concerned, the batter is only there to protect the fish. Obviously you can use any kind of boneless fish you can lay your hands on. **Tony**

Serves 4

vegetable oil for deep-frying
350g/12oz monkfish fillet, cut into
    4cm/1¹/₂in cubes
4 tablespoons plain flour

For the batter:
100g/3¹/₂oz plain flour
100g/3¹/₂oz cornflour
pinch of salt
1 egg, beaten
300ml/ ¹/₂ pint milk

Prepare the batter by mixing together the plain flour, cornflour and salt in a large bowl. Make a well in the centre and add the egg. Gradually whisk the egg into the flour and then slowly add the milk, whisking all the time, until you have a smooth batter.

Heat the vegetable oil in a large, deep saucepan or a deep-fat fryer until it is hot enough to brown a cube of bread in 1 minute. Pat the monkfish dry on kitchen paper and dust it lightly with the flour, shaking off any excess. Dip it in the batter and then deep-fry for 1¹/₂ minutes, until golden brown. Drain on kitchen paper and serve with home-made chips (see page 56).

Lasagne al ragu di carne

Lasagne with meat sauce

I can't stand the way the English make lasagne – all béchamel and meat sauce. You may as well be eating shepherd's pie. Here the pasta (all seven or eight layers of it) is the equal star, and the sauce is there just to add interest, not to smother the whole thing. If you want to, you can use ready-made pasta but it won't be as good. **Giorgio**

Serves 6

1 quantity of Giorgio's pasta dough
   (see page 244) or 500g/
   1lb 2oz bought fresh
   lasagne sheets
75g/3oz Parmesan cheese,
   freshly grated
sea salt and freshly ground black
   pepper

2 garlic cloves, crushed
500g/1lb 2oz minced beef
1 sprig of rosemary
1 sprig of sage
2 bay leaves
150ml/¼ pint red wine
1 tablespoon tomato purée
200g/7oz can of plum tomatoes

For the meat sauce:
1 tablespoon olive oil
1 onion, finely chopped
1 carrot, finely chopped
1 celery stalk, finely chopped

For the white sauce:
50g/2oz butter
50g/2oz plain flour
600ml/1 pint milk
pinch of freshly grated nutmeg

To make the meat sauce, heat the olive oil in a saucepan, add the onion, carrot and celery and sweat over a low heat for 3–4 minutes. Add the garlic, minced beef and herbs and cook until the meat is browned all over. Add the red wine and bubble until completely evaporated, then season with salt and pepper. Stir in the tomato purée and plum tomatoes, plus 2 tomato tins full of water. Bring to the boil, then reduce the heat to very low, cover and simmer for 2 hours, stirring every 10–15 minutes or so. Adjust the seasoning if necessary, then remove from the heat and allow to cool slightly.

    Now make the white sauce. Melt the butter in a saucepan and stir in the flour. Cook over a medium heat for 3–4 minutes, stirring all the time, then gradually add the milk, stirring well between each addition. Bring to the boil, stirring constantly, and simmer for 2 minutes. Remove from the heat, season with salt, pepper and the nutmeg and pass through a fine sieve. Set aside in a warm place.

    If using home-made pasta, cut the dough into quarters and pass each piece through a pasta machine on the widest setting, then fold it in half and repeat, each time switching the machine down a setting, and dusting with flour if necessary, until you reach the finest setting. If you are rolling the dough by hand, aim for a thickness of 0.5mm. Cut the pasta into long strips about the size of your hand.

Cook the pasta in a large pan of boiling water for 1 minute, then drain, refresh under cold water, drain again and pat dry.

Preheat the oven to 180°C/350°F/Gas Mark 4. Cover the bottom of a large ovenproof dish with a couple of tablespoons of each sauce. Cover with a single layer of pasta sheets, then with a couple more tablespoons of each sauce. Keep layering in this way until you have about 7–8 layers of pasta and sauces, finishing with a layer of white sauce. Sprinkle the Parmesan on top and bake for about 35 minutes, until golden and bubbling.

Easy spaghetti bolognese
Spaghetti Bolognese all'Inglese

I know this is going to give Giorgio the heebie-jeebies (something I love to do) but what it lacks in Italian authenticity it makes up for with its unabashed kid and grown-up appeal. You can make this with any meat you have around – beef, pork, lamb or even sausagemeat. Just don't invite Giorgio to dinner, or you'll get a lecture about what is true Italian cuisine and what is bastardised English food! **Tony**

Serves 4

2 tablespoons olive oil
1 large onion, finely chopped
2 carrots, finely chopped
2 garlic cloves, finely chopped
4 smoked streaky bacon rashers, chopped
450g/1lb lean minced beef

2 x 400g/14oz cans of chopped tomatoes
2 tablespoons Worcestershire sauce
350g/12oz spaghetti
sea salt and freshly ground black pepper
freshly grated Parmesan cheese, to serve

Heat the oil in a saucepan, add the onion, carrots, garlic and bacon and cook for 5 minutes, until the vegetables have softened. Add the mince and cook, stirring occasionally, for 5 minutes, until browned. Stir in the chopped tomatoes and Worcestershire sauce and simmer for 10–15 minutes, until slightly thickened. Season to taste.

Cook the pasta in a large pan of boiling, salted water until *al dente*, then drain well and return to the pan. Pour in the sauce, toss together and divide between 4 bowls. Sprinkle over plenty of Parmesan and serve.

Chicken schnitzel

Pollo 'Milanese'

I've borrowed liberally here from the Milanese, who are experts at crumbing and frying their meat. The idea is to bash the chicken out so it's very thin, then you really get the impact of the crisp fried breadcrumb coating. Kids love the crunch. With any luck, they'll even eat their vegetables too. **Tony**

Serves 4

4 boneless, skinless chicken breasts
plain flour for dusting
2 eggs, beaten
125g/4oz fresh white breadcrumbs
4 tablespoons sunflower oil

For the spaghetti:
1 tablespoon olive oil

1 onion, chopped
1 garlic clove, crushed
400g/14oz can of chopped tomatoes
1 tablespoon tomato purée
350g/12oz spaghetti
sea salt and freshly ground black
pepper

Put the chicken breasts between 2 pieces of clingfilm and bash with a meat mallet or rolling pin until they are about 1cm/½in thick. Dust the chicken with plain flour, shaking off any excess. Put the beaten eggs in a shallow dish and spread the breadcrumbs out on a plate. Coat the chicken breasts in the egg and then in the breadcrumbs, making sure they are completely covered. Cover and chill until ready to use.

To make the spaghetti, heat the oil in a saucepan, add the onion and fry for 3–4 minutes, until softened. Add the garlic and cook for a minute longer, then add the tomatoes, tomato purée and some seasoning. Bring to the boil, reduce the heat and simmer for 10–15 minutes, until thickened. Meanwhile, cook the spaghetti in a large pan of boiling salted water for 8–10 minutes, until *al dente*.

Heat the sunflower oil in a large frying pan and add the chicken. Fry for 4–5 minutes on each side over a fairly gentle heat, until golden and cooked through. Drain the spaghetti, toss with the tomato sauce and adjust the seasoning. Serve with the chicken.

Giorgio's pizza

Forget your sad and sorry takeaway pizzas, with their swamps of melted cheese and thick, chewy crust. Real Italian pizza is very light and digestible. The base should be thin and you should never overload it with too many ingredients. Italian 'oo' flour is a very fine flour used by Italians for making pizza and pasta, and can be found in large supermarkets and Italian delis. Once you've got your base, you can add any number of different toppings. Here's my version, followed by Margherita's, Charlee's, Jack's and Hollie's. **Giorgio**

Serves 4

For the dough:
650g/1lb 5oz Italian 'oo' flour
7g sachet of Easyblend yeast
2 teaspoons salt
25ml/1fl oz olive oil
50ml/2fl oz warm milk
325ml/11fl oz warm water

For the tomato topping:
**2 x 400g/14oz cans of plum
    tomatoes**
¹/₂–1 teaspoon dried oregano

4 garlic cloves, crushed
6 tablespoons olive oil
pinch of sugar (optional)
**sea salt and freshly ground black
    pepper**

To finish the pizza:
anchovy fillets in oil
pitted black olives
mozzarella cheese, roughly chopped
basil leaves

To make the dough, mix the flour, yeast and salt together in a large mixing bowl and stir in the olive oil and milk. Gradually add the water, mixing well to form a soft dough. Turn the dough out on to a floured work surface and knead for about 5 minutes, until smooth and elastic. Transfer to a clean bowl, cover with a damp tea-towel and leave to rise for about 1¹/₂ hours, until doubled in size.

Meanwhile, make the topping. Tip the plum tomatoes into a bowl and crush them with a fork. Stir in the oregano, garlic, olive oil and some salt and pepper. Taste and add the sugar if it is too acidic.

Preheat the oven to its highest setting. Punch down the risen dough, divide it into 4 and roll out each piece into a rectangle or circle about 5mm/¹/₄in thick. Transfer to baking tins or pizza tins (you will probably have to cook them in batches). Spoon the tomato mixture on top, leaving a border round the edge, then sprinkle over some anchovies and black olives. Scatter the mozzarella over the top and bake for about 10–12 minutes, until the base is golden brown. Remove from the oven, sprinkle with basil leaves and serve.

Margherita's pizza	**Charlee's pizza**	**Jack's pizza**	**Hollie's pizza**
no tomato topping	no tomato topping	tomato topping	tomato topping
mozzarella cheese	sliced cooked potato	blanched spinach	sliced mushrooms
pieces of Parma ham	rosemary sprigs	ricotta cheese	mozzarella cheese
	sea salt	a little mozzarella cheese	basil leaves
	drizzle of olive oil	olives	

Fish pie
Torta di pesce

A great way to introduce children to fish. Texturally this dish is a dream, with its fluffy mash top and creamy filling. In reality it's just a fish version of shepherd's pie, but it's creamier and a lot more interesting. **Tony**

Serves 4

450g/1lb haddock fillet, skinned
125g/4oz smoked haddock fillet, skinned
300ml/½ pint milk
100g/3½oz chestnut mushrooms, sliced
25g/1oz butter
1 onion, finely chopped
50g/2oz plain flour
2 small eggs, hard-boiled, shelled and quartered

50g/2oz cooked peeled prawns
2 tablespoons chopped parsley
sea salt and freshly ground black pepper

For the topping:
675g/1½lb floury potatoes, peeled and cut into chunks
2 tablespoons milk
50g/2oz Cheddar cheese, grated
knob of butter

Preheat the oven to 200°C/400°F/Gas Mark 6. Cut the fresh and smoked haddock into large pieces, place in a frying pan and pour over the milk. Add the mushrooms and bring to the boil, then cover and remove from the heat. Set aside for 10 minutes, then lift the fish out of the milk with a slotted spoon and set aside, reserving the milk and mushrooms.

Melt the butter in a large pan, add the onion and cook over a gentle heat for 5 minutes. Add the flour and cook, stirring for 1 minute. Remove from the heat and gradually stir in the reserved milk and mushrooms. Return to the heat and bring to the boil, stirring constantly, until it becomes a smooth, thickened sauce. Simmer for 3 minutes, then remove from the heat.

Stir the fish into the sauce with the eggs, prawns, parsley and some seasoning. Spoon the mixture into a 1.8 litre/3 pint ovenproof dish and set aside.

For the topping, cook the potatoes in boiling salted water until tender. Drain well and mash until smooth, then stir in the milk, cheese and butter and adjust the seasoning. Using a fork, spread the potato over the fish and sauce. Bake for 20 minutes, until the top is golden.

Petto di pollo al marsala

Chicken breast with marsala

Traditionally this dish is made with lemon, but because of Margherita's allergies we had to look for another way of doing it. The sweetness of marsala is a great hit with kids. By boiling it you get rid of the alcohol, leaving just that nice sweetness and stickiness. But don't let that stop you serving it for a dinner party, either! **Giorgio**

Serves 4

2 boneless, skinless chicken breasts
50g/2oz plain flour
1 tablespoon olive oil
75ml/2½fl oz marsala

25g/1oz butter
sea salt and freshly ground black
pepper

Cut each chicken breast in half horizontally and season with salt and pepper. Dust with the flour and shake off any excess.

Heat the olive oil in a large frying pan and add the chicken. Cook for 5–6 minutes, until golden underneath, then turn the chicken over and add the marsala. Bring to a simmer and let the alcohol bubble and reduce for a minute or two.

Remove the chicken from the pan and keep warm. Toss the butter in the flour left from coating the chicken and add to the pan. Return the chicken pieces to the pan and stir them around, until the butter has melted and the flour has cooked, which will take a minute or two. Place the chicken breasts on warmed serving plates and strain the sauce over the top.

Tuna burger

'Hamburger' di tonno

With help from Christian Delteil, my partner at Bank, we developed this burger especially for fish! diners. It is my attempt to bring a little class back into the burger. It looks like a burger, feels like a burger, but the overall experience is so much more satisfying. And you can still feel good about yourself after you've eaten it. **Tony**

Serves 4

500g/1lb 2oz fresh tuna
4 tablespoons tartare sauce
4 burger buns, split
handful of shredded iceberg lettuce
2 tablespoons mayonnaise

tomato ketchup
2 tomatoes, sliced
2 gherkins, finely sliced
sea salt

Chop the tuna as finely as possible, so it is almost minced. Put it in a bowl, add the tartare sauce and a good pinch of sea salt and mix well. Separate the mixture into 4 portions and shape into burgers by pressing together gently. Place on a baking tray, cover with clingfilm and chill for at least 15 minutes.

When ready to serve, heat a ridged grill pan until very hot and cook the tuna burgers on it for 3–4 minutes per side, until scored with marks from the grill (or you can cook them in a little oil in a large frying pan). Remove from the grill pan.

Lightly toast the burger bun halves. Place the shredded lettuce in a small bowl and mix with the mayonnaise. Spoon the mixture on to the bottom halves of the burger buns, top with the tuna burgers, then spread some tomato ketchup on the burgers. Top with the sliced tomatoes, add more ketchup, then add the gherkins. Add the bun tops and serve.

Salsicce con polenta

Sausages with polenta

Here are the two greatest staples of Italian cooking, brought together in one of the easiest dishes you'll ever make. You could call it the Italian equivalent of toad in the hole. Not that I would. But you could. **Giorgio**

Serves 4

125g/4oz polenta
1 litre/1³/₄ pints milk
200ml/7fl oz double cream

1 teaspoon salt
500g/1lb 2oz Italian pork sausages

Put the polenta in a large jug so that you can pour it easily. Bring the milk and cream to the boil in a large saucepan and add the salt. Slowly add the polenta in a continuous stream, stirring with a long-handled whisk all the time, until completely blended. As soon as the polenta starts to bubble, reduce the heat to as low as possible and cook for 20 minutes, stirring to make sure it doesn't stick.

Meanwhile, cook the sausages on a barbecue, in the oven or in a frying pan until sizzling and cooked through. Pour the polenta on to 4 warmed plates and arrange the sausages on top.

Insalata verde con Parmigiano

Parmesan and cos lettuce salad

I originally came up with this as an answer to the craze for rocket and Parmesan salad that spread through just about every restaurant in the Western world. Cos, or romaine, is very much cheaper than rocket, so you get all the flavour without breaking the bank. Any resemblance between this and an American Caesar salad is purely intentional. **Giorgio**

Serves 4

2 cos lettuces
25g/1oz Parmesan cheese,
  freshly grated

For the dressing:
2 organic egg yolks
1 tablespoon Dijon mustard

1 garlic clove, finely chopped
100ml/3½fl oz sunflower oil
100ml/3½fl oz groundnut oil
2 tablespoons white wine vinegar
2 tablespoons water
sea salt and freshly ground black
  pepper

To make the dressing, put the egg yolks, mustard and garlic in a bowl and beat together with a little salt and pepper. Add the oils a drop at a time, whisking constantly, until you have a thick, glossy mayonnaise-style emulsion (when about a third of the oil has been incorporated, you can start to add it a little more quickly). Thin the mixture with the white wine vinegar and water and adjust the seasoning to taste.

Chop the lettuces roughly and place in a large serving bowl. Add the dressing and toss together well. Sprinkle over the Parmesan cheese, then taste and adjust the seasoning if necessary.

Sausage and pea risotto

Risotto con salsicce e piselli

For me, this is a logical progression from bangers and mash, and shows just how much the Italian influence is creeping into the British kitchen. Despite being a risotto, however, it tastes more British than Italian, which probably has a lot to do with the chipolata sausages. **Tony**

Serves 4–6

16 chipolata sausages

1.2 litres/2 pints chicken stock

2 tablespoons olive oil

knob of butter

1 onion, finely chopped

1 garlic clove, crushed

400g/14oz risotto rice

450g/1lb fresh or thawed frozen peas

25g/1oz Parmesan cheese,
    freshly grated

sea salt and freshly ground black
    pepper

Preheat the oven to 200°C/400°F/Gas Mark 6. Place the chipolata sausages in a roasting tin and bake for 20–25 minutes, until golden and cooked through. Remove from the oven and cut into quarters.

Put the stock in a saucepan and keep it at simmering point. Heat the oil and butter in a large, heavy-based saucepan until the butter is foaming, then add the onion and cook gently for about 5 minutes, until softened. Add the garlic and rice and cook, stirring, for a few minutes until the rice is shiny and opaque. Add the hot stock a ladleful at a time, allowing it to be absorbed by the rice before adding more, and stirring constantly. The whole process will take about 20 minutes. When you are about to add the last ladleful of stock, tip in the peas and chipolata sausages at the same time, then cook for about 5–6 minutes longer, until the liquid has been absorbed.

When the rice feels soft and fluffy and the texture is creamy but each grain is still firm to the bite in the centre, the risotto is ready. Remove from the heat and leave to rest for 30 seconds, then stir in the Parmesan cheese. Season well to taste and serve immediately.

Torta di cioccolata alla Margherita

Margherita's eggless chocolate cake

Plaxy made this for our daughter, Margherita, who is not able to eat eggs. One day, she asked me if the pizza Margherita was named after her. I would have liked to say yes, but due to the fact that it was named after Queen Margherita of Italy in 1889, I couldn't. Now at least she can tell everybody there is a chocolate cake named after her. **Giorgio**

Serves 8

450g/1lb plain flour (organic if
    possible)
6 tablespoons unsweetened cocoa
    powder (Green and Black's
    is good)
2 teaspoons baking powder
2 teaspoons bicarbonate of soda
300g/10oz caster sugar
125ml/4fl oz vegetable oil
300ml/ $^1/_2$ pint water
2 tablespoons distilled white vinegar
2 teaspoons vanilla extract
whipped cream, to decorate

For the icing:
'It's all mine' dark chocolate spread
    by English Provender Company
OR
225/8oz icing sugar
25g/1oz unsweetened cocoa powder
75g/3oz butter, diced
1 tablespoon golden syrup
4 tablespoons milk

whipped cream, to decorate

Preheat the oven to 180°C/350°F/Gas Mark 4. Sift the flour, cocoa powder, baking powder and bicarbonate of soda into a large bowl and stir in the sugar. Combine all the wet ingredients in another bowl. Pour the wet ingredients into the dry ingredients all at once and beat until smooth. Pour the batter into a greased 23cm/9in springform cake tin and bake for about 1 hour, until a skewer inserted in the centre comes out clean (place a sheet of foil over the top of the cake if it becomes too dark). Remove from the oven and leave to cool in the tin.

Turn the cake out of the tin and spread the 'It's all mine' chocolate spread over the top. Or, if you are making your own icing, sift the icing sugar and cocoa powder into a bowl and make a well in the centre. Gently heat the butter, golden syrup and milk until the butter has melted, then pour into the well in the dry ingredients and stir until smooth. Beat with a wooden spoon until the icing has cooled and thickened slightly. Spread the icing over the top and sides of the cake with a palette knife. Decorate with whipped cream.

Locobocker glory

Giorgio and I wanted to come up with a real treat that children would love at the end of a meal. The inspiration for it comes from the knickerbocker glories and banana splits that I used to have at greasy spoon caffs when I was a kid – only this one tastes better. **Tony**

Serves 4

125g/4oz caster sugar
200ml/7fl oz water
juice of 1 lemon
2 small pears, peeled, cored and
    sliced
250g/9oz raspberries
2 tablespoons icing sugar
200g/7oz strawberries, halved if
    large

4 scoops of vanilla ice-cream
4 scoops of chocolate ice-cream
300ml/½ pint double cream,
    whipped

To serve:
4 wafers
a little grated chocolate

Put the sugar and water in a large, shallow pan and stir over a gentle heat until the sugar has dissolved. Add the lemon juice and pears, cover the pan and simmer for 5–10 minutes, until the pears are just tender. Remove them from the pan with a slotted spoon and set aside to cool. Increase the heat under the pan and boil the liquid, uncovered, for 10–15 minutes, until slightly syrupy. Remove from the heat and allow to cool completely.

Whiz the raspberries and icing sugar in a food processor until smooth, then strain through a sieve. Reserve 4 strawberries for decoration. Divide the rest of the strawberries and the pears between 4 sundae glasses and spoon over a little of the cold sugar syrup. Top with a scoop of ice-cream and drizzle over some of the raspberry sauce. Top with the remaining ice-cream and sauce. Spoon the whipped cream on top and decorate with the wafers, reserved strawberries and grated chocolate.

Feeding friends

Let them come into the kitchen. Better still, throw them an apron and give them a job to do. **Tony**

giorgio

You know the worst thing about being a chef? Nobody ever asks me round to dinner. Ever! Basically, everyone is scared of cooking for me because they think I only ever eat the sort of food I cook in the restaurant, and that I would turn my nose up at anything simple. Which, of course, is absolutely ridiculous.

I would love to be asked to dinner. I love home cooking, and I love the idea of catching up with people in their own environment. It's not just about food, it's about friendship and fun, and drinking wine and meeting people on their own ground.

I've been to some homes where we ate some very nice meals – all very professional and well presented – yet I never got the impression that our hosts were happy to see us. They seemed very tense, and preoccupied with the food. That's just not right.

I'd rather eat a good home-cooked stew or a simple roast and just feel relaxed and have fun. I must be the easiest guest in the world to please. For me, it's special just being able to sit down to eat. As a chef, you don't often get to eat sitting down. You're always standing or moving, snacking on bits and pieces when you can, then, more often than not, you have to pick up a takeaway on the way home. I remember when I was cooking at Zafferano, I once went six whole months without ever sitting down to eat a meal. So for me, it's a luxury.

These days we're always feeding people at our place. Not big, pre-planned dinner parties that you go and shop for specially, but the kids bring friends over, or Plaxy's parents drop in. There are always people hanging around at dinner time (hmmm, funny that), so my natural instinct is to feed them.

I think Italians are born to feed people. They love asking people to dinner. To an Italian, the best thing you can possibly do for somebody is cook for them. When you have someone in your house, you are stripping yourself down in front of them. You are showing them who you really are. In Italy, I get lots of invitations to dinner because nobody worries about looking bad. All they care about is being a good host, and giving you the sort of food they like to eat.

In fact, I think one of the reasons they like to ask me over for dinner is because they think they can teach me something. And you know what? I always learn something.

tony

The simple truth is that we try too hard to impress when we have people over to dinner. We buy all the cookbooks, we watch all the celebrity chefs on televison, we write lists, we angst out like crazy and then try to turn ourselves into three-starred Michelin chefs overnight, without the advantage of a twenty-strong kitchen brigade, a dozen burners, and twenty years of solid, on-the-job training. The stress and strain of making the big effort usually means we wind up so spun out that by the time we finally get to put dinner on the table, the last thing we want to do is eat anything.

The trick is to expect less of ourselves, and remember that they're coming over for a nice night out and a bit of a laugh. If they want a full-on gourmet experience, then they can book a table at Gordon Ramsay's restaurant, or Michel Roux's, or Heston Blumenthal's.

So we have to do what we can to defuse any expectations of formality and grandeur. For example, ask them to come the following week, not two months ahead. Ask them to supper rather than a dinner party, so they get the idea it will be more congenial. Or try asking them to come midweek instead of on a Saturday, so they know they can't stay all night.

There are not a lot of skills required to feed somebody well. Do a nice soup, put out some crusty bread and make a green salad, and you're half-way there.

The stress and strain of making the big effort usually means we wind up so spun out that by the time we finally get to put dinner on the table, the last thing we want to do is eat anything.

On the practice

tony

Let's get dinner parties into perspective. Fifty per cent is about the people, the talk, the fun and the socialising; twenty-five per cent is about the booze, and twenty-five per cent is about the food.

When you look at it like that, it doesn't sound at all scary. And the honest truth is, it isn't. So the thing to do is relax. Why go running around like a headless chicken, trying to find something wildly impressive to cook for your guests, when you probably already have a couple of killer dishes that you could make standing on your head, blindfolded, with one hand tied behind your back?

Ideally, the food you give your guests should be saying something about you. A meal cooked from a book has one flavour, but a meal cooked from the heart has a totally different flavour altogether. With home cooking, the most important thing is to make the dish feel as if it's yours.

The same logic can be used when working out what wine you're going to serve. Too many people try to turn themselves into instant wine buffs, and end up buying wines that are meant to impress but turn out to be totally inappropriate. Start with what you like. If you really fancy that Gamay you bought at the supermarket, and you like what happens when you chill it lightly and drink it with fish, then do it.

Now this doesn't mean that if your guests turn up with something good to drink, you can just pop it away in a cupboard. At least ask them if they would like to open it now, or be gracious and do it anyway. Involve your guests as much as you can.

Let them come into the kitchen while you're cooking. Better still, throw them an apron and give them a job to do. There's nothing better than the feeling that you're all in it together, and it really helps everyone to relax. And why shouldn't they relax? After all, your house is not a restaurant – and there's no bill to pay at the end of the evening.

Rule number one is to spend as much time as possible with your guests. After all, they've come to see you, not your fancy plating technique.

The worst thing you can do is have people over for dinner and then go and hide in the kitchen, while they're sitting at the table wondering where you are.

A good plan is to do one dish that you can finish off on the spot and work on while everybody's around, but to prepare the other dishes ahead so you only have to warm them, carve them or unmould them. You could have a cold starter in the fridge, for instance, a whole fish or chicken roasting in the oven, and then finish off the zabaglione on the spot, so it's nice and warm and fresh.

I would hate it if you cooked for me and couldn't sit down with me to eat. I'd rather we just had a sandwich together. After all, the great thing about entertaining people in your home is conviviality. It's all about sharing – sharing your time, your conversation, your food and your wine. What you're really doing is sharing yourself.

To help this along, I always like the idea of serving something big, like a sea bass or a salmon, which you can put down in the middle of the table. I like putting out plates and letting everyone choose what they want. You're not a chef, you don't run a restaurant, so you don't have to plate everything individually.

When my grandmother used to cook, she would bring out the main dish and put it down on the table. Maybe it would be a big joint of roast veal, roughly cut into good chunky pieces. Your own plate would always be put in front of you, warm and clean. Then the dishes of vegetables would go down – maybe spinach with butter, or peas, and potatoes, and a big jug of sauce, or *mostarda di frutta*, those wonderful preserved fruits from Cremona in northern Italy. Suddenly the table would be smiling, and smelling fantastic. That's how to turn a dinner into a feast that everybody can share.

giorgio

Recipes
Feeding friends

Zuppa pavese

Savoury toasts

Risotto Milanese

Grilled stuffed mussels

Pizzoccheri

Whole stuffed turbot with Parmesan beans

Branzino al forno in crosta di sale e erbe

Oxtail braised in Burgundy

Lamb Wellington

Anatra con lenticchie

Baccala in umido

Lemon tart

Zabaglione

Sticky toffee pudding

Zucotto

Zuppa pavese

Soup with bread and poached eggs

This Lombardian speciality is a simple peasant dish, devised to use up stale bread. Yet when we were kids brought up on minestrone, we always thought of it as a special treat. My grandmother would only ever make it when she had some chicken stock that she thought was really, really good. **Giorgio**

Serves 4

1 quantity of Giorgio's chicken stock
    (see page 241)
50g/2oz butter
8 thick slices of stale country bread

8 eggs
4 tablespoons freshly grated
    Parmesan cheese
salt

Reheat the stock, seasoning well with salt to taste.

Heat the butter in a large frying pan, add the bread and fry gently on both sides until crisp and golden (do this in batches if necessary). Divide the slices between 4 deep soup plates and gently break an egg on top of each slice. Sprinkle over the grated Parmesan. Slowly pour the hot stock into the soup plates, taking care not to pour it directly on top of the eggs. Serve immediately.

Savoury toasts
Crostini

These were inspired by the wonderful bruschetta that I've often watched Giorgio make, but the influences at work here are French (tapenade and anchoïade) and English (smoked trout pâté). The toasts work as an appetiser, nibbles with drinks or as a full-blown starter. Because they can be prepared ahead of time, they are a totally non-stress option. **Tony**

Serves 6–8

1 large sourdough loaf, thinly sliced
sea salt and freshly ground black
    pepper

For the tapenade:
225g/8oz pitted black olives
1 garlic clove, peeled
25g/1oz walnuts
juice of ½ lemon
100ml/3½fl oz extra virgin olive oil
small bunch of flat-leaf parsley,
    roughly chopped

For the anchoïade:
50g/2oz anchovies in olive oil,
    drained
1 small red onion, roughly chopped
1 garlic clove, roughly chopped
1 egg, hard-boiled, shelled and
    finely chopped
1 teaspoon white wine vinegar

For the smoked trout pâté:
2 hot-smoked trout fillets
1 teaspoon creamed horseradish
juice of ½ lemon
½ cucumber, peeled and roughly
    chopped

For the tapenade, place the olives and garlic in a food processor and blitz for a few seconds until roughly chopped. Add the walnuts and lemon juice and blitz again. Season to taste with salt and pepper, then, with the machine running, add the olive oil through the feeder tube until you have a rough paste. Stir through the parsley and set aside.

For the anchoïade, place the anchovies in the cleaned bowl of the food processor and blitz for a few seconds with the red onion and garlic. Add the hard-boiled egg and white wine vinegar and pulse for a few seconds to make a rough paste. Season to taste with salt and pepper.

For the smoked trout pâté, place the trout fillets in the cleaned bowl of the food processor and blitz with the creamed horseradish and lemon juice. Add the cucumber, blitz again for a few seconds and then season well to taste.

Toast the sourdough bread slices on both sides. Allow to cool and harden a little before spreading one third with the tapenade, one third with the anchoïade and one third with the smoked trout pâté. Serve on a large platter.

Risotto Milanese

Saffron risotto

In Milan this rich, creamy risotto with its sunny golden colour and bitter tang of saffron normally comes with osso buco attached. While they are made for each other, I find the risotto also works extremely well on its own as an elegant and sophisticated starter. **Giorgio**

Serves 4

900ml/1½ pints chicken stock
3 pinches of saffron strands,
    steeped in 2 tablespoons
    boiling water
75g/3oz butter
1 small onion, finely chopped
1 slice of veal bone marrow, about
    4cm/1½in thick
300g/10oz superfine carnaroli
    risotto rice
175ml/6fl oz white wine

25g/1oz Parmesan cheese, freshly
    grated
sea salt and freshly ground black
    pepper

For the bone marrow:
4 slices of veal bone marrow,
    about 2cm/¾in thick
3 tablespoons mixed fresh white
    breadcrumbs and grated
    Parmesan cheese

Preheat the oven to 180°C/350°F/Gas Mark 4. Place the 4 slices of bone marrow in a small baking tin, sprinkle the Parmesan and breadcrumbs over them and place in the oven for about 25 minutes, until brown on top (if necessary, keep pouring off the excess fat from the baking tin).

Meanwhile, put the stock in a pan with the saffron liquid and keep it at simmering point. Melt 50g/2oz of the butter in a large, heavy-based pan, add the onion and the marrow from the bone and cook gently until the onion is very soft but not browned. Add the rice and cook, stirring, over a medium heat until it is coated with the butter. Pour in the white wine and simmer until it has been absorbed by the rice. Add the hot stock a ladleful at a time, stirring well between each addition and waiting until three-quarters of the liquid has been absorbed before adding more. After about 15–20 minutes, when the rice is tender and moist and all the stock has been added, remove from the heat and leave to rest for 30 seconds. Dice the remaining butter and stir it in, together with the grated Parmesan. Season to taste with salt and pepper.

Transfer the risotto to 4 warmed serving bowls. The consistency should be *all' onda* – which means that when you tilt the bowl the risotto should move like a wave. Garnish with the slices of bone marrow and serve straight away.

Grilled stuffed mussels

Cozze ripiene alla griglia

The presentation alone makes this a winner, served on the half shell in a gorgeous tomatoey sauce. All the real work (not that there's much of it) can take place beforehand, so all you have to do is pop the filled shells under the grill when your guests arrive. **Tony**

Serves 4 as a starter

36 largish live mussels
4 tablespoons white wine
1 plump garlic clove, peeled
4 tablespoons roughly chopped
    flat-leaf parsley
6 sunblush (semi-dried) tomatoes

grated zest of 1 lemon
50g/2oz fresh white breadcrumbs
1 tablespoon olive oil
sea salt and freshly ground black
    pepper

Wash and scrub the mussels, pulling out any beards and discarding any that have opened. Place the mussels in a large pan with the wine and cover with a tight-fitting lid. Cook over a high heat for a minute or two, shaking the pan from time to time, until the mussels have just opened. Strain the liquid from the pan into a small bowl and set the mussels aside to cool, discarding any that have not opened.

For the topping, place the garlic, parsley, tomatoes and lemon zest in a small food processor and pulse until finely chopped. Add the breadcrumbs, olive oil, a little salt and pepper, and 3–4 tablespoons of the reserved mussel liquor and pulse again until smooth.

When the mussels are cool enough to handle, snap off and discard the top half of each shell. Arrange the mussels on a baking sheet and spoon a little of the topping over each. Place under a hot grill or in a hot oven for 2–3 minutes, until bubbling and golden. Serve at once.

Pizzoccheri

Buckwheat pasta with potato, cabbage and fontina

Pizzoccheri is a pasta from the mountainous Valtellina region of Lombardy. It is like tagliatelle in shape but is an earthy brown colour because it is made with buckwheat flour, and is much more robust and chewy. Traditionally accompanied by cabbage, potatoes and cheese, it serves as a very practical form of internal heating during the bitter northern Italian winters. Save it for a cold winter's night with friends.

If you don't want to make your own pasta, you can buy dried pizzoccheri from some Italian delis. **Giorgio**

Serves 6

150g/5oz buckwheat flour
600g/1lb 5oz Italian 'OO' flour
1½ teaspoons salt
5 eggs
100ml/3½fl oz warm milk

For the sauce:
1 small Savoy cabbage, diced
1 medium potato, peeled and diced

125g/4oz butter
2 leeks, finely chopped
2 sage leaves
100g/3½oz Parmesan cheese,
    freshly grated
175g/6oz fontina cheese, diced
salt and freshly ground black
    pepper

To make the pasta, put the two flours and the salt in a bowl or food processor and mix in the eggs and milk a little at a time until the mixture forms a firm dough. Turn out on to a work surface and knead for 3–5 minutes, until smooth, then wrap in clingfilm and chill for 1 hour.

Roll the dough out very thinly, either using a pasta machine or with a rolling pin. Cut into ribbons about 2cm/³/₄in wide.

Cook the cabbage in a pan of boiling salted water for 1 minute, then drain and refresh under cold running water. Add the diced potato to a small saucepan of boiling salted water, cook until very tender, then drain well, reserving a cupful of the cooking water.

Heat about 25g/1oz of the butter in a frying pan, add the leeks and cook gently until tender. Season well. Heat the remaining butter in a large frying pan and add the cabbage, leeks, potato, reserved potato water (this acts as a thickening agent) and sage leaves. Heat gently.

Meanwhile, bring a large pan of water to the boil, add the pasta and cook for 1–2 minutes, until just tender. Drain and add to the cabbage and potatoes. Cook for 3 minutes until the liquid has almost evaporated, then remove from the heat and stir in the Parmesan and fontina cheese. Season to taste and leave to rest for a few moments before serving.

Whole stuffed turbot with Parmesan beans

Rombo ripieno e fagiolini al Parmigiano

This has dinner party written all over it, but that doesn't mean it's a fiddly or fancy dish. Far from it. About the only tricky bit is getting the whole fish into your oven. The mushroom stuffing and the creamy sauce add a bit of finesse, but basically it's the fish itself that's the star, which is how it should be. **Tony**

Serves 6–8

1 x 3kg/7lb turbot, descaled and boned (ask your fishmonger to do this)
large knob of butter
2 celery stalks, chopped
1 shallot, chopped
1 leek, chopped
small bunch of parsley, roughly chopped
small bunch of chervil, roughly chopped
3 tablespoons vermouth, such as Noilly Prat
300ml/½ pint fish stock
100ml/3½fl oz double cream

sea salt and freshly ground black pepper

For the stuffing:
25g/1oz butter
2 shallots, finely chopped
1kg/2¼lb chestnut mushrooms, finely chopped
3 tablespoons double cream

For the Parmesan beans:
350g/12oz green beans
2 shallots, finely chopped
50g/2oz Parmesan cheese, finely grated

Preheat the oven to 180°C/350°F/Gas Mark 4. To make the stuffing, melt the butter in a frying pan and cook the shallots in it for a few minutes until softened. Add the mushrooms and cook until they release their juices. Continue to cook until the liquid has evaporated, then stir in the cream. Season well and spoon into the cavity of the turbot.

Place a large roasting tin on the hob and heat the knob of butter in it. Add the celery, shallot, leek, parsley and chervil and cook for just a few minutes. Pour over the vermouth and stock and bring to the boil. Lay the turbot on top of the vegetables and put the roasting tin straight into the oven. Bake for 10 minutes, then cover with foil and bake for a further 30 minutes. Transfer the turbot to a serving dish, cover and keep warm.

Place the roasting tin back on the hob and simmer until the liquid has reduced by half. Add the cream and heat through. Strain the sauce through a sieve, then set aside and keep warm.

Bring a small pan of salted water to the boil and plunge in the green beans. Cook for no more than 2 minutes, then drain and toss with the chopped shallots and the Parmesan. Serve the turbot at the table with the green beans, and drizzle with the sauce.

Branzino al forno in crosta di sale e erbe

Whole sea bass roasted in a salt and herb crust

This is not just a wonderful dish, it's also a wonderful piece of theatre. When you bring the whole fish to the table and break open the crust to reveal the tender steamed fish beneath, it's like showtime. Don't be surprised if everyone stands up and starts applauding. **Giorgio**

Serves 6

350g/12oz mixed soft herbs, such as
    chives, chervil, parsley and basil
1kg/2¹/₄lb sea salt
1kg/2¹/₄lb plain flour
7 medium egg whites

50ml/2fl oz water
1 x 1.8kg/4lb sea bass, gutted
    and descaled
extra virgin olive oil, to serve

Put the herbs in a food processor and whiz to a paste. Mix them with the salt and leave to rest in the fridge overnight.

The next day, preheat the oven to 220°C/425°F/Gas Mark 7. Take the salt and herb mixture out of the fridge and mix with the flour, egg whites and water to form a dough. Roll out the dough to about 5mm/¹/₄in thick. Cut out a rectangular piece, about 4cm/1¹/₂in bigger than the fish, and lay the sea bass on it. Cut out another rectangle of dough, large enough to cover the fish, lay it on top of the fish and press to seal the edges of the 2 pieces of dough. Cut away any excess from the edges. Place on a baking sheet and bake for 30 minutes.

To serve, transfer the fish to a large platter and take a hammer wrapped in a clean cloth with you to the table. Crack open the crust and show your guests the fish, then lift the fillets off the bone. Serve with a light drizzle of extra virgin olive oil.

Oxtail braised in Burgundy

Coda di bue brasato al vino rosso

Oxtail is one of those timeless things that is never actually the height of fashion yet never really goes out of fashion either. Restaurants tend to go fancy and take all the meat off the bone before reassembling it, but I think that cuts out half the fun, which is slurping the meat off the bones. This is definitely a hands-on dish, best shared with people you can make a mess with. **Tony**

Serves 4

1 large oxtail, cut into 5cm/2in pieces
4 tablespoons olive oil
4 sprigs of thyme
small bunch of flat-leaf parsley,
**   chopped**
2 tablespoons plain flour
1.2 litres/2 pints beef stock
125g/4oz bacon lardons
175g/6oz button onions, peeled
2 tablespoons sugar

sea salt and freshly ground black
**   pepper**

For the marinade:
1 bottle of good red wine, such as
**   Pinot Noir**
1 large onion, roughly chopped
1 leek, roughly chopped
2 carrots, roughly chopped
2 celery stalks, roughly chopped
6 black peppercorns

Place the oxtail in a large shallow dish, pour over the wine and add all the other marinade ingredients. Cover and leave to marinate in the fridge overnight.

The next day, drain the oxtail, reserving the marinade, and pat dry with kitchen paper. Heat half the oil in a large saucepan, add the oxtail and brown all over until almost caramelised. Strain the vegetables from the marinade and add to the pan with the thyme and parsley. Stir in the flour, then gradually add the strained marinade and the stock. Cover tightly and leave to simmer gently for about 5 hours, until the oxtail is so tender it is almost falling off the bone. Remove from the heat, take the oxtail out of the sauce with a slotted spoon and keep warm. Put the pan back on the hob and bring to the boil. Simmer until the liquid is reduced by half, pressing the vegetables against the side of the pan to release all the flavour.

Meanwhile, heat the remaining oil in a frying pan, add the lardons and fry until crisp and golden. Remove from the pan and set aside. Add the button onions to the pan and cook for 10 minutes, until golden all over. Sprinkle over the sugar and cook for a further 5 minutes, until caramelised and tender.

Taste the sauce and season with salt and pepper if needed. Strain through a sieve and return to the pan, then add the lardons and onions and heat through gently. Serve the oxtail with the sauce on a pile of creamy mashed potato.

Lamb Wellington

Agnello alla 'Wellington'

Here I've taken the beef Wellington concept, changed the beef to lamb and cut the whole thing down to a more manageable size. The best part comes when you bring the 'surprise packets' to the table and cut through to reveal the layers of spinach, aubergine and mushroom and the lightly pink, tender lamb within. **Tony**

Serves 4

4 tablespoons olive oil
2 best ends of lamb, each weighing about 200g/7oz (the cannon from the eye of the meat)
large knob of butter
175g/6oz chestnut mushrooms, finely chopped
8 sunblush (semi-dried) tomatoes, finely chopped
1 small aubergine, finely chopped

1 plump garlic clove, finely chopped
3 anchovy fillets, finely chopped
250g/9oz large spinach leaves
2 x 375g/13oz packets of ready-rolled puff pastry
1 large egg, beaten
sea salt and freshly ground black pepper

Preheat the oven to 200°C/400°F/Gas Mark 6.

Heat half the olive oil in a large frying pan over a high heat and sear the lamb all over until browned. Remove from the pan and set aside. Add the remaining oil and the butter to the pan and heat until the butter is foaming. Stir in the mushrooms, sunblush tomatoes and aubergine and cook for about 15 minutes, until browned and very tender. Stir in the garlic and anchovies and season to taste. Cook for a further 10 minutes, until the mixture has a soft, paste-like consistency. Remove from the heat and set aside.

Wash the spinach leaves and place them in a saucepan with just the water that clings to the leaves. Cook gently until just wilted, being careful not to break the leaves. Drain well and leave to cool.

Place the ready-rolled puff pastry on a work surface. Open out the spinach leaves and lay them out over the rolled-out pastry. Then spread the mushroom and aubergine paste all over the spinach layer. Finally, put a piece of lamb on each one and fold over the pastry to make a neat parcel. Pinch the edges together to seal, then trim off any excess pastry. Brush with the beaten egg and place on a baking tray. Allow to rest in the fridge for 10 minutes or so. Bake for 20–25 minutes, until the pastry is crisp and golden. To serve, thickly slice the lamb Wellingtons.

Anatra con lenticchie
Duck with lentils

This is not a traditional dish but something I thought up to cook at home one day. Plaxy's mother had just given us a fabulous *cocotte* (casserole dish) and I wondered what I could cook in it that would be special. This is a great one-pot dish, even if I do say so myself. **Giorgio**

Serves 4

1 duck, weighing about 1.4kg/3½lb
350g/12oz Italian brown lentils
2 tablespoons olive oil
50g/2oz pancetta, finely chopped
4 garlic cloves, chopped
2 small carrots, finely chopped
1 large onion, finely chopped

2 celery stalks, finely chopped
1 tablespoon chopped flat-leaf
   parsley
1 bay leaf
100ml/3½fl oz white wine
sea salt and freshly ground black
   pepper

Remove any excess fat from the duck. Cook the lentils in plenty of boiling water for 25–30 minutes, then drain and set aside. Heat the olive oil in a large casserole, add the pancetta, garlic, carrots, onion, celery and parsley and sweat over a gentle heat until the onion is translucent. Add the duck and bay leaf and brown the duck all over in the hot fat. Pour in the wine and allow to bubble for a few minutes to evaporate the alcohol. Add 200ml/7fl oz water and mix well. Cover the pan and cook for about 1–1¼ hours, then add the drained lentils and cook for a further 15 minutes, or until the duck is done. Season to taste, then take out the duck, cut it into rough pieces and serve with the lentils.

Baccala in umido

Salt cod stew

I love the flavour of salt cod – it is so intense and distinctive, yet at the same time it feels comforting and familiar. Buy it dried from an Italian, Spanish or Portuguese specialist, and soak it overnight to reconstitute it. This dish is a definite for entertaining because you can do it all beforehand and then just heat it up in the oven when everybody arrives. **Giorgio**

Serves 4

2 tablespoons olive oil
400g/14oz onions, finely sliced
400g/14oz can of plum tomatoes
800g/1³/₄lb salt cod, soaked in
    cold water overnight
sunflower oil for deep-frying

50g/2oz plain flour
50g/2oz pine nuts, toasted
50g/2oz sultanas
sea salt and freshly ground black
    pepper

Heat the olive oil in a saucepan, add the onions and sweat over a gentle heat for 5–6 minutes, until translucent. Add the tomatoes and simmer gently for 15 minutes. Meanwhile, drain and rinse the cod, cut it into 4 pieces and pat dry with kitchen paper.

Heat the sunflower oil to 180°C/350°F in a deep-fat fryer or a large, deep saucepan. Dust the pieces of cod with the flour, shaking off any excess, and drop them into the hot oil. Fry for 2 minutes, until lightly coloured, then remove with a slotted spoon and transfer to the tomato sauce. Mix well and simmer for 15 minutes. Stir in the pine nuts and sultanas and heat through. Check and adjust the seasoning before serving.

Lemon tart

Torta di limone

Tarte au citron, to give it its fancy French name, was THE restaurant dessert of the late Eighties and Nineties, thanks to the fine pastry skills of the kitchens of the Roux brothers, Marco Pierre White and Gordon Ramsay. In short, the dish is a classic. Luckily, it's actually a doddle for the home cook, so don't feel you need three Michelin stars before attempting it. **Tony**

Serves 6

3 eggs
40g/1¹/₂oz caster sugar
juice and grated zest of 2 medium
     lemons
100ml/3¹/₂fl oz whipping cream
icing sugar for dusting

For the pastry:
150g/5oz plain flour
50g/2oz caster sugar
75g/3oz unsalted butter, cut into
     cubes
2 egg yolks
1 egg white, lightly beaten

To make the pastry, sift the flour into a large bowl, make a well in the centre and add the sugar, butter and egg yolks. Work with your fingertips so that the butter and egg yolks are first rubbed into the flour and sugar, then worked together to form a ball of dough – it must be smooth and pliable, not crumbly. Wrap the dough in clingfilm and chill for about 45 minutes.

Preheat the oven to 190°C/375°F/Gas Mark 5. Roll out the pastry on a lightly floured surface and use to line a 20cm/8in loose-bottomed tart tin. Prick the base lightly with a fork and chill again for about 20 minutes. Line with greaseproof paper, fill with dried beans and bake for 15 minutes. Remove the greaseproof paper and beans and bake for a further 5 minutes. Brush the pastry lightly all over with the beaten egg white to seal it and then return to the oven for 1 minute. Remove from the oven and leave to cool.

Reduce the oven temperature to 120°C/250°F/Gas Mark ¹/₂. For the filling, lightly whisk together the eggs, sugar, lemon juice and zest. Whip the cream until fairly stiff, then gradually whisk it into the egg mixture. Pour the filling into the pastry case and bake for 30 minutes. Leave to cool, then remove the tart from the tin and serve dusted with icing sugar.

Zabaglione

Marsala egg custard

Apparently this was invented accidentally when the chef of Carlo Emmanuel I of Savoy poured sweet wine into an egg custard by mistake. The dish was a hit, and an Italian classic was born. There's a fair amount of beating involved here, so why not get your guests working, by taking turns with the whisk, preferably in time to some good Italian opera. And don't forget to keep half an egg shell when you separate the eggs – you'll need it for measuring the Marsala. **Giorgio**

Serves 4

4 egg yolks
4 tablespoons caster sugar

Marsala wine

Put the egg yolks and sugar in a large heatproof bowl and whisk with an electric hand-held beater until pale and thick. Add 4 half egg shells of Marsala and sit the bowl over a pan of gently simmering water, making sure the water doesn't touch the base of the bowl. Continue whisking until the mixture is pale and very foamy and has increased dramatically in volume – this will take at least 10 minutes. Ladle into glasses and serve immediately. Zabaglione is usually served with dry Italian biscuits such as cantuccini.

Sticky toffee pudding

Budino al caramello

Sticky toffee pudding might have been born and bred in England, but it has since conquered most of the English-speaking world. You'll find it everywhere from New York to New Zealand, while in Australia it's almost impossible to find a restaurant that doesn't have it on the menu. You won't find *that* happening with an Italian *zucotto*, now, will you? **Tony**

Serves 6–8

125g/4oz pitted dates, finely chopped
50g/2oz dried apricots, finely chopped
300ml/½ pint boiling water
1 teaspoon bicarbonate of soda
75g/3oz unsalted butter
100g/3½oz caster sugar
50g/2oz light muscovado sugar

1 teaspoon vanilla extract
2 eggs
175g/6oz self-raising flour

For the toffee sauce:
125g/4oz light muscovado sugar
50g/2oz unsalted butter
100ml/3½fl oz double cream
½ teaspoon vanilla extract

Preheat the oven to 180°C/350°F/Gas Mark 4. Put the dates and apricots in a small saucepan, pour over the boiling water and bring back to the boil. Simmer for 2–3 minutes, until the dried fruit is soft, then remove from the heat and stir in the bicarbonate of soda. Leave to cool a little.

Beat the butter and sugars together until light and fluffy, then add the vanilla extract. Beat in the eggs one at a time, adding a little of the flour with each egg. Sift in the remaining flour and fold it in gently, followed by the dried fruit and its liquid. Pour the mixture into a greased 23cm/9in square shallow cake tin and bake for about 30 minutes, until the pudding is risen and brown and a skewer inserted in the centre comes out clean.

While the pudding is baking, make the toffee sauce. Put all the ingredients in a saucepan and heat gently, stirring occasionally, until the sugar and butter have melted. Bring to the boil and let it bubble for 1 minute.

When the pudding is done, prick it all over with a skewer and spoon about a quarter of the toffee sauce over it. Return it to the oven for about 30 seconds, then remove and cut into squares. Serve each portion with some extra toffee sauce poured over – plus lots of cream or vanilla ice-cream if you like.

Zucotto

Chocolate, cream and nut cake

This dome-shaped 'cake' with its filling of nuts, chocolate and cream represents one of the high points of Tuscan desserts, and to my mind is far more interesting than the ubiquitous *tiramisu*. There is a fair amount of work involved here, but the result is spectacular, to say the least. **Giorgio**

Serves 8

200g/7oz dark chocolate (70 per cent cocoa solids)
4 tablespoons cognac
4 tablespoons Vin Santo
1 litre/1³/₄ pints double cream
75g/3oz blanched almonds, roughly chopped
75g/3oz blanched hazelnuts, roughly chopped
150g/5oz icing sugar

25g/1oz cocoa powder

For the sponge:
6 eggs, separated
150g/5oz icing sugar
1 tablespoon honey
75g/3oz cornflour
75g/3oz plain flour, plus extra for dusting
melted butter for brushing

Preheat the oven to 190°C/375°F/Gas Mark 5. First make the sponge. Put the egg yolks, icing sugar and honey in a large bowl and beat with an electric hand-held beater until pale and thick. In a separate bowl, whisk the egg whites until they form stiff peaks. With a large metal spoon, carefully fold them into the egg yolks. Sift in the cornflour and plain flour and fold them in too.

Brush a 20cm/8in square cake tin with melted butter and dust with flour. Pour the cake mixture into the tin and bake for about 30 minutes, until golden and springy to the touch. Turn the sponge out on to a wire rack and leave to cool.

Finely chop the chocolate and leave 150g/5oz of it in the fridge. Put the rest in a bowl set over a pan of gently simmering water. Turn off the heat and set aside to melt.

When the sponge is cool, cut off the crusty edges and cut the cake into slices about 1cm/¹/₂in thick. Use to line a round bowl, 1.5 litres/2¹/₂ pints in capacity, making sure the cake comes all the way up to the top. Mix the cognac and Vin Santo together and, using a pastry brush, gently brush them over the cake.

Whip the double cream until stiff, stir in the nuts and finely chopped chocolate and divide this mixture in half. Stir the melted chocolate into one half. Place this mixture in the bottom of the cake-lined bowl and smooth the surface with a spoon. Fill the bowl to the top with the other cream mixture and then place a serving plate on top. Turn the bowl and plate upside down and chill in the fridge for at least 1 hour. Lift off the bowl, leaving the pudding on the plate, and dust with the icing sugar and cocoa powder. Cut into wedges to serve.

Leftovers

I bet the Italians could even turn these leftover recipes into leftovers.
Giorgio

tony

I bet very few cookbooks have a chapter of recipes for leftovers, but it's something that means a lot to both Giorgio and myself. For every recipe in this book, there are probably another five recipes dying to get out. By that I mean that once you've cooked a dish you have created the raw materials with which you can go and cook another one.

As far as I'm concerned, leftovers are among the great glories of the kitchen. The only pity is the use of the word 'leftovers', which makes them sound like second-class citizens. Nothing could be further from the truth. Perhaps we should bring back the French word *rechauffé*, which was so popular in the Victorian era. It literally means reheated, but it does sound a bit more upmarket than leftovers.

I was brought up not to waste anything. When I cook roast lamb, I'm not even thinking about the meal I'm having that night. Instead, I'm thinking about Monday's cold lamb, fat chips and pickles, Tuesday's lamb sandwiches and Wednesday's shepherd's pie. The thing is, each of these is a great dish in its own right. Just because it's moved further along the food chain, it doesn't mean it has deteriorated in quality.

Every country has its own repertoire of leftover dishes, but few can come close to good old British ingenuity. Bubble and squeak, for instance, may have started life as a fry-up of leftover potatoes, onions and Brussels sprouts or cabbage, but you can play with any number of variations on a theme and produce a thing of great beauty. Flip back to my Scallops with Bacon and Bubble and Squeak on page 48 and you'll see what I mean. Kedgeree was once just a misguided attempt to recreate an original Indian dish, but it's a fantastic way of using up leftover smoked fish or steamed rice.

The Italians often use their leftovers to stuff pasta, the Dutch and the Germans turn them into croquettes, the Chinese turn them into a stir-fry, and we British will, generally speaking, wrap them in pastry. When in doubt, we make a good old-fashioned pie, pasty or tart.

The whole idea of knowing you're getting two or three meals out of one dish is a bit of a buzz. We Brits are proud of our frugality – particularly the generation that lived through the last world war and its attendant food rationing – and we should all have a good, basic understanding of how to make something out of not much at all.

For me, just the knowledge that I'm putting something to good use instead of wasting it actually makes the meal taste better.

giorgio

Like Tony, I don't like the term 'leftovers'. In Italian cooking there's no such thing as leftover food, just food that hasn't been used up yet. Everything gets used sooner or later, absolutely everything. We can't stand the thought of a single morsel going to waste.

In the UK, we are obsessed with cooking at the last minute, or *à la minute*. Anything left over is looked down upon. Restaurants are often the worst offenders, responsible for some terrible wastage. As a chef, I hate it when restaurants throw out enormous amounts of food at the end of the day. I think it is disgusting and lazy, and should not be allowed.

In my kitchen, very little goes in the bin. One chef might look at a chicken or a duck and see just a seared chicken breast or confit duck leg, whereas the first thing I see is all that wonderful cooking fat, which can be rendered down and used later for crisping potatoes, or sautés. Then I see the stock you can make from the bones, for use in soups and sauces, the skin that could be crisped and served as a garnish, and so on. It's the same at home; I'm always trying to work out what else I can do with what is left.

Leftovers account for some of the greatest dishes in the Italian repertoire. Look at the classic Tuscan *ribollita*, a soup of bread and vegetables. That dish represents Italian culture all over the world, but it owes its existence to good old leftover bread. And if you still have some bread left over after your *ribollita*, you can make a chunky, rustic Panzanella salad (see page 88), in which the bread comes alive in the juices of tomatoes, olive oil and vinegar, or a velvety *pappa al pomodoro*, a gloriously thick tomato and bread soup that represents childhood in a bowl to most Florentines.

I can never understand why people throw their old bread out and then go to the supermarket and pay good money for inferior commercial breadcrumbs. I think they are completely mad!

Pasta and rice are also fabulous as so-called leftovers. While Northern Italians love their risotto, they love it even more the second time around, when it can be shaped into rounds and fried into a crisp-crusted *saltati*. Or they deep-fry it in big, golden, crumbed balls known as *arancini* (oranges), or smaller balls filled with mozzarella cheese, known as *suppli telefoni*, or 'telephone wires', because the cheese melts and forms into long strings when you bite into it. Leftover spaghetti can be mixed with eggs and shaped into a spaghetti omelette, or mixed with leftover sauce, topped with cheese and baked in the oven.

If Italians didn't make the most of their leftovers, I think most Italian cookery books would be only half as long. I bet they could even turn these leftover recipes into leftovers.

Recipes
Leftovers

Pea and ham soup

Tagliatelle con il sugo d'arrosto

Risotto al salto

Fishcakes

Salt beef hash

Zucchini ripieni

Stir-fried noodle kedgeree

Polpette di tacchino agrodolce

An Englishman's Peking duck

Welsh rarebit croquettes

Polenta pasticciata

Pasta 'ncaciata

Lamb sandwich

Agnolini con ripieno di stugato

Pea and ham soup

Zuppa di piselli e garretto di maiale

It's worth making friends with your local delicatessen, so you can talk them into giving you their leftover ham bone when they've finished carving all the meat off it. Otherwise, a good, meaty ham hock will do just as nicely. **Tony**

Serves 4

large knob of butter
1 large onion, finely chopped
small bunch of flat-leaf parsley,
    plus extra to serve
small bunch of mint, plus extra
    to serve

150g/5oz green split peas
1 ham bone
1.2 litres/2 pints ham stock or water
150g/5oz fresh or frozen peas
sea salt and freshly ground black
    pepper

Heat the butter in a large saucepan, add the onion and cook gently for about 8 minutes, until beginning to soften. Tie the parsley and mint together with string and add to the pan. Add the split peas, stirring to coat them with the onion and butter mixture, and cook for a minute or two. Add the ham bone and stock, bring to the boil and simmer gently for about 20 minutes. Stir in the fresh or frozen peas and cook for about 20 minutes longer, until the split peas are completely tender.

Remove the ham bone and herbs and purée the soup either with a hand-held blender or in a jug blender. Season well to taste.

Ladle the soup into warmed soup bowls and serve with flakes of meat from the ham bone and an extra sprinkling of finely chopped mint and parsley.

Tagliatelle con il sugo d'arrosto
Tagliatelle with juices from the roast

Whenever you roast a joint of meat – pork, beef or lamb – you release those fabulous, sticky juices that are left on the bottom of the tin. For an Italian, there could be no better destiny for these juices than to finish up as a simple, yet totally satisfying sauce to serve with tagliatelle, fettuccine or pappardelle. Even just a few tablespoons of the juices will turn plain old tagliatelle into something robust and delicious. Traditionally, this dish is served before the meat itself. **Giorgio**

Serves 4

cooking juices left over from the
    roast
50ml/2fl oz olive oil
1 sprig of rosemary
1 sprig of sage

1 garlic clove, crushed
500g/1lb 2oz tagliatelle
25g/1oz Parmesan cheese, freshly
    grated

Heat the juices from the roast in the roasting tin or a large saucepan with half the oil, the rosemary, sage and garlic. Let the herbs fry gently in the oil for a couple of minutes. Meanwhile, cook the tagliatelle in a large pot of boiling salted water until *al dente* – tender but still firm to the bite. Drain well, reserving a little of the cooking water. Add the pasta to the roast juices and stir to combine. Add the rest of the oil and the Parmesan and mix well. If the pasta seems too dry, add a little of the cooking water just before serving.

Risotto al salto

Fried risotto cakes

Freshy made risotto is one of the truly great Italian dishes, but I get just as excited about left-over risotto, because then I can have another great Italian dish – a delicious crisp rice cake. Just the natural starch of the rice is enough to keep the cake together. The trick here is to keep the heat low and cook it nice and slow, then add your toppings. **Giorgio**

2 tablespoons olive oil

leftover risotto (risotto Milanese is ideal)

Heat 2 tablespoons of olive oil over a high heat in a small, heavy-based frying pan, about 15–18cm/6–7in in diameter. Add leftover risotto Milanese (see page 198) or any other leftover risotto and press it down so it forms a thick cake. Reduce the heat and fry for 4–5 minutes, until the risotto is crisp and golden underneath. Turn over and cook the other side until gold-en. Serve plain or with a topping of your choice – for example, freshly grated Parmesan cheese; thinly sliced mozzarella with diced tomoato and basil; ricotta cheese and chopped cooked spinach.

To make individual risotto cakes, grease a non-stick muffin tin very generously with butter and put some risotto into each compartment, pressing it down with a spoon to make patties. Remove from the tin and cook as above.

Fishcakes

Crocchette di pesce

This is everything that is great about British comfort food, all tamped down into a nice round patty, covered in breadcrumbs and fried until golden brown. While I've described how to do the potato from scratch here, leftover mashed potato will do equally well. **Tony**

Serves 4

450g/1lb floury potatoes, such as Maris Piper or King Edward, peeled and cut into chunks
350g/12oz salmon tail fillet, skinned
350g/12oz smoked haddock fillet, skinned
300ml/½ pint milk
1 large bunch of coriander, chopped

50g/2oz Japanese panko breadcrumbs, or other natural golden breadcrumbs
1 egg, beaten
2 tablespoons sunflower oil
450g/1lb baby spinach leaves
sea salt and freshly ground black pepper

Put the potatoes in a saucepan, cover with water and bring to the boil. Simmer until tender, then drain well and return to the pan. Place over a gentle heat to dry out the potatoes and then mash well until smooth. Season to taste and remove from the heat.

Put the salmon and smoked haddock in a large frying pan and cover with the milk. Bring to the boil, then cover with a lid and turn off the heat. Leave for 5 minutes, until the fish is cooked through, then take it out of the milk and leave to cool. Flake the cooled fish and carefully fold it into the mashed potato, along with the chopped coriander and plenty of seasoning. Shape into 4 large fishcakes and place on a baking tray lined with clingfilm. Chill for 30 minutes.

Spread the breadcrumbs out on a plate. Brush the fishcakes with the beaten egg and then dip them in the breadcrumbs, completely covering them. Heat the oil in a large frying pan and cook the fishcakes for about 3 minutes on each side, until crisp and golden.

Meanwhile, place the spinach in a large saucepan with a little water and cook until just wilted. Drain well and season to taste. Serve the fishcakes with the wilted spinach. They are very good with a little beurre blanc, too – made like the one on page 63 but omitting the mustard and herbs.

Salt beef hash

Polpettone di manzo saltato

I really like salt beef (or corned beef) served with carrots and a little of the stock in which it was cooked. Which is just as well, because I really, really like this terrific salt beef hash you can make the next day. This is my idea of leftover heaven. **Tony**

Serves 4

3 tablespoons olive oil
1 onion, finely chopped
200g/7oz leftover salt beef, cut into cubes
175g/6oz leftover cooked carrots, roughly chopped

250g/9oz leftover cooked potatoes, diced
4 eggs
freshly ground black pepper

Heat 2 tablespoons of the oil in a large frying pan, add the onion and cook for about 6 minutes, until softened. Add the salt beef, carrots and potatoes and cook for 5–8 minutes, until golden. Meanwhile, heat the remaining oil in a separate pan and fry the eggs. Season the hash with a good grinding of black pepper and serve with the fried eggs.

Zucchini ripieni

Stuffed courgettes

This is a recipe I got from my grandmother, who used to make it whenever she had some left-over bread and meat. Practically any kind of meat will work here. Serve as a starter, lunch or picnic dish. **Giorgio**

Serves 4

50g/2oz butter
250g/9oz leftover roast meat, such
    as lamb, pork or beef,
    minced or finely chopped
200g/7oz tomatoes, skinned,
    deseeded and diced
25g/1oz parsley, chopped

50g/2oz fresh breadcrumbs
50g/2oz Parmesan cheese, freshly
    grated
4 medium-sized, straight courgettes
50ml/2fl oz olive oil
sea salt and freshly ground black
    pepper

Preheat the oven to 180°C/350°F/Gas Mark 4. Melt the butter in a saucepan, add the meat and heat gently for a few minutes. Add the tomatoes and cook gently until pulpy. Transfer to a bowl and stir in the parsley, breadcrumbs and three-quarters of the Parmesan. Season to taste.

    Cut the courgettes in half lengthways and, using a spoon, scrape out the white part from the inside. Put the hollowed-out courgettes in a roasting tin, drizzle with the oil and bake for 10 minutes. Fill with the stuffing mixture and sprinkle with the remaining Parmesan. Bake for 15 minutes, until the cheese is golden and the courgettes are tender.

Stir-fried noodle kedgeree

Taglierini e pesce saltati alla cinese

Okay, so it's not really a kedgeree, which is officially made with rice. But the principle of using spiced-up leftover smoked fish is pretty much the same, and whatever it is, it tastes delicious.
Tony

Serves 4

225g/8oz dried egg noodles
25g/1oz butter
2 tablespoons olive oil
bunch of spring onions, finely chopped
pinch of dried chilli flakes
250g/9oz leftover cooked salmon, smoked haddock, fresh haddock, prawns, etc.

2 eggs, beaten
large bunch of coriander, finely chopped
small bunch of flat-leaf parsley, finely chopped
sea salt and freshly ground black pepper

Place the egg noodles in a large bowl, cover with boiling water and leave to soak for 10 minutes. Heat the butter and oil in a wok or large frying pan, add the spring onions and chilli flakes and fry for a few minutes. Stir in the leftover fish and toss together gently for a few minutes to heat through. Drain the noodles well and add to the pan, tossing everything together. Finally add the beaten eggs, herbs and seasoning and toss again. The heat from the noodles should just cook the eggs. Remove from the heat and serve immediately.

Polpette di tacchino agrodolce

Turkey meatballs in sweet and sour sauce

This is one way of solving that old what-on-earth-am-I-going-to-do-with-the-Christmas-turkey dilemma. The little meatballs are good just as they are but really turn into something special when combined with the agrodolce (sweet and sour) sauce. You can make these with any lefover white meat actually, so don't feel you have to wait until Boxing Day! **Giorgio**

Serves 4

50g/2oz stale country-style bread
2 tablespoons milk
300g/10oz cooked turkey, minced or
    very finely chopped
200g/7oz boiled potatoes, mashed
50g/2oz Parmesan cheese, freshly
    grated
2 small eggs
1 garlic clove, crushed
25g/1oz parsley, chopped
grated zest of 1 small lemon
100g/3½oz breadcrumbs
100ml/3½fl oz sunflower oil

sea salt and freshly ground black
    pepper

For the sauce:
200ml/7fl oz olive oil
2 juniper berries
2 bay leaves
2 white onions, thinly sliced
100ml/3½fl oz white wine vinegar
50g/2oz sultanas, soaked in warm
    water for 10 minutes, then
    drained

Cut off the crusts from the bread and soak the bread in the milk. Meanwhile, put the minced turkey in a bowl with the potatoes and mix well with a wooden spoon. Add the Parmesan, eggs, garlic, parsley, lemon zest and some salt and pepper and stir well until the mixture comes together. Squeeze out the soaked bread, add to the mixture and give it a good stir. Shape the mixture into 12 small balls with your hands and flatten them so they look like mini burgers. Chill for about 30 minutes.

Meanwhile, make the sauce. Put the olive oil in a pan with the juniper berries and bay leaves and heat gently so that it becomes infused with the flavours. Add the onions and cook for about 20 minutes, until very tender. Add the white wine vinegar and sultanas and cook for 2 minutes longer. Remove from the heat and leave to cool.

Coat the meatballs in the breadcrumbs. Heat the sunflower oil in a large frying pan, add the meatballs and fry gently for about 5 minutes on each side, until golden and cooked through. Drain on kitchen paper and place on a baking tray. Pour the sauce over the meatballs and leave to infuse for 1 hour before serving.

An Englishman's Peking duck
Anatra alla Pechinese

The original Peking duck recipe takes two days and involves bicycle pumps and lots of basting. This is simpler, faster, but no less delicious. You can find Mandarin pancakes in the frozen food section of some large supermarkets. **Tony**

Serves 4 as a starter

4 poached duck legs (see Wild
    duck with orange, grapefruit
    and beetroot on page 107)
duck fat (see Wild duck with
    orange, grapefruit and
    beetroot on page 107)

For the plum sauce:
450g/1lb red plums, stoned and
    chopped
2 shallots, finely chopped

50ml/2fl oz red wine vinegar
50g/2oz light muscovado sugar
1 star anise
sea salt and freshly ground black
    pepper

To serve:
1 packet of Mandarin pancakes
1 cucumber, cut into thin batons
1 bunch of spring onions, cut
    lengthways into fine shreds

Preheat the oven to 170°C/325°F/Gas Mark 3. Place the duck legs in a shallow ovenproof dish and add the reserved duck fat. Cover with foil, place in the oven and cook for 1 hour, until the meat is very tender and falling away from the bone.

To make the plum sauce, place all the ingredients in a heavy-based saucepan and simmer for 15–20 minutes, until pulpy and thickened. Remove from the heat and set aside.

Shred the meat from the duck legs. Heat the pancakes according to the instructions on the packet. To serve, let everyone fill their own pancakes with shredded duck, cucumber, spring onions and plum sauce, then roll them up to eat with their fingers.

Welsh rarebit croquettes

Crochette di eglefino al formaggio

This is what is known in the trade as lateral thinking. All I've done is start with the under-lying principles of Welsh rarebit, turned the bread into the breadcrumbs, added a bit of smoked haddock, then kicked it along with a little cayenne pepper. **Tony**

Serves 4

50g/2oz butter
50g/2oz plain flour
150ml/¼ pint milk
275ml/9½fl oz Mackeson's ale or
    stout
50g/2oz mature Cheddar cheese,
    grated
¼ teaspoon cayenne pepper
250g/9oz cooked smoked haddock,
    flaked

To finish the croquettes:
4 tablespoons plain flour
1 egg, beaten
50g/2oz fresh white breadcrumbs
    (made from bread that is 2–3
    days old)
large knob of butter
2 tablespoons olive oil

Heat the butter in a medium saucepan until foaming, then sprinkle over the flour. Whisk the flour into the butter until it forms a thick paste. Gradually pour in the milk and the Mackeson's, whisking all the time over a gentle heat. Bring to the boil and simmer for a few minutes, until you have a thick, smooth sauce. Remove from the heat and beat in the cheese and cayenne pepper, then stir in the smoked haddock. Set aside, cover and leave to cool completely. Chill for at least 2 hours.

Mould the mixture into 8 croquette shapes. Spread the flour out on a plate, put the beaten egg in a shallow bowl and the breadcrumbs in another. Dip the croquettes in the flour, then roll them in the beaten egg and finally coat with the breadcrumbs. Place on a baking tray and leave in the fridge to firm up for at least 20 minutes.

Heat the butter and oil in a large frying pan and cook the croquettes for 4–5 minutes, until golden and crisp all over.

Polenta pasticciata
Baked polenta

Where I come from, polenta always means hard polenta – that is, polenta that has been left to set rather than served soft and runny. When hard polenta cools, it is easy to cut into slices, which can then be layered with just about anything you have on hand and put in the oven to heat through. If you have any leftover polenta, use it here rather than making the polenta from scratch. **Giorgio**

Serves 6

125g/4oz polenta
1.2 litres/2 pints milk
300g/10oz mozzarella cheese, diced
50g/2oz Parmesan cheese, freshly
    grated
50g/2oz butter
sea salt and freshly ground black
    pepper

For the meat sauce:
25g/1oz dried porcini mushrooms
2 tablespoons olive oil
1 onion, finely chopped

1 carrot, finely chopped
1 celery stalk, finely chopped
250g/9oz minced beef
200g/7oz can of chopped tomatoes
1 glass of white wine

For the béchamel sauce:
600ml/1 pint milk
½ onion
8 black peppercorns
1 bay leaf
50g/2oz butter
50g/2oz plain flour

Put the polenta in a large jug so that it can be poured in a steady stream. Bring the milk to the boil in a large saucepan, add 1 teaspoon of salt and then slowly add the polenta in a continuous stream, stirring with a long-handled whisk all the time, until completely blended. When the polenta starts to bubble, reduce the heat as low as possible and cook for 20 minutes, stirring occasionally. Pour it into a baking tray in a layer at least 1cm/½in thick and leave to cool.

Meanwhile, make the meat sauce. Put the porcini in a bowl, pour over enough hot water to cover and leave to soak for 20 minutes. Heat the oil in a large saucepan, add the onion, carrot and celery and cook for about 8 minutes, until softened. Add the minced beef and cook, stirring, for 2–3 minutes, until browned. Add the tomatoes and wine and simmer to allow the alcohol to evaporate. Season with salt and pepper.

Drain the porcini, squeezing out any excess liquid, then chop them and add to the sauce. Cook for a further 25–30 minutes, until you have quite a dry sauce. Taste and adjust the seasoning.

For the béchamel, put the milk in a pan with the onion, peppercorns and bay leaf and bring just to boiling point. Remove from the heat, cover and leave to stand for 10 minutes for the flavours to infuse the milk. Melt the butter in another saucepan and whisk in the flour to make a sandy-coloured paste. Remove the pan from the heat and gradually strain in the hot milk, whisking constantly. Return to the heat and whisk until the sauce thickens, then simmer gently for 2–3 minutes. Season to taste with salt and pepper.

Preheat the oven to 200°C/400°F/Gas Mark 6. To assemble the dish, cut the polenta into thin strips. Spread a layer of meat sauce and then of béchamel over the base of a large ovenproof dish. Arrange half the strips of polenta on top, spreading more of the meat sauce and béchamel between each strip. Sprinkle over half the mozzarella and Parmesan and then repeat with the remaining polenta and sauces. Top with the remaining mozzarella and Parmesan, dot the butter on top and bake for 20 minutes, until the top is golden and bubbling.

Pasta 'ncaciata
Pasta-stuffed aubergines

A fantastic way to use up leftover spaghetti or penne. This is one of those great dishes that are easy and likeable enough to make a no-fuss family supper but also impressive enough to serve at a dinner party. **Giorgio**

Serves 4

4 aubergines
3 tablespoons olive oil
1 small onion, finely chopped
2 garlic cloves, crushed
400g/14oz can of chopped tomatoes
1 bay leaf
400g/14oz (cooked weight) leftover pasta

150g/5oz ball of mozzarella cheese, diced
large handful of basil, roughly torn
large handful of flat-leaf parsley, finely chopped
25g/1oz Parmesan cheese, freshly grated
sea salt and freshly ground black pepper

Preheat the oven to 200°C/400°F/Gas Mark 6. Place the aubergines on the rack in the oven and bake for 25–30 minutes, until they are completely tender. Leave to cool.

Meanwhile, heat the olive oil in a saucepan, add the onion and cook gently for 5 minutes, until softened. Add the garlic, tomatoes and bay leaf and simmer for 20 minutes, until the sauce has thickened. Season well to taste.

Halve the aubergines lengthways, leaving the stalks in place. Scoop out the flesh into a large bowl and mash with a fork. Toss with the cooked pasta, tomato sauce, mozzarella, basil and parsley. Season with salt and pepper to taste.

Spoon the pasta mixture into the aubergine shells and place in a roasting tin. Scatter the Parmesan on top and bake for 10 minutes, until the filling has heated though and the cheese has melted.

Lamb sandwich

Panino d'agnello

Leftover lamb is one of my favourite ingredients. After all, without it, you wouldn't have shepherd's pie. But if you want to do something with leftover lamb that's a bit different, and really, really easy, then this is the one. **Tony**

Serves 4

1 aubergine, thinly sliced
2 large courgettes, thinly sliced
1 sweet potato, thinly sliced
4 tablespoons olive oil
150g/5oz plain yoghurt
small bunch of mint, chopped

1 ciabatta loaf
4 tablespoons mint sauce
8 large slices of cooked lamb
6 sunblush (semi-dried) tomatoes
sea salt and freshly ground black
 pepper

Preheat the oven to 200°C/400°F/Gas Mark 6. Arrange the aubergine, courgette and sweet potato slices in a single layer in a large roasting tin (you may have to use 2 roasting tins to accommodate all the vegetables). Brush with the olive oil and roast for 30–35 minutes, until tender and golden.

Mix together the yoghurt and mint, seasoning well with salt and black pepper.

Slice the ciabatta horizontally in half and toast it. Brush with the mint sauce and top one half with half the sliced lamb. Season with salt and pepper, then spread over half the yoghurt dressing and top with half the roasted vegetables and sunblush tomatoes. Repeat with the remaining ingredients and then top with the other half of the ciabatta. Press down well, cut into quarters and serve.

Agnolini con ripieno di stugato

Agnolini pasta stuffed with stew

The English regard leftover stew as the remnants of a meal but we Italians see it as the beginning of another meal. With this method, you can take virtually any leftover meat stew, mince it, combine it with Parmesan and egg and use it as a pasta filling. If, however, your family is like mine and you rarely have any stew left over, you can make this very special filling from scratch. **Giorgio**

Serves 4

300g/10oz beef (from the leg or
    flank)
2 garlic cloves, peeled and cut into
    slivers
75g/3oz butter
1 onion, chopped
250ml/9fl oz white wine
75g/3oz pancetta, diced
1 plain pork sausage
75g/3oz Parmesan cheese, freshly
    grated

1 egg, plus a little beaten egg, for
    brushing
freshly grated nutmeg
1 quantity of Giorgio's pasta dough
    (see page 244)
2 litres/3$\frac{1}{2}$ pints Giorgio's chicken
    stock (see page 241)
sea salt and freshly ground
    black pepper

Make some small slits in the beef with the point of a sharp knife and insert a garlic sliver in each one. Heat half the butter in a heavy-based saucepan, add the onion and sweat until tender. Place the beef on top, season with salt and pepper, then add a few tablespoons of the white wine and cover the pan. Cook very gently for 2 hours, until the meat is very tender, adding a little more wine every 30 minutes or so to prevent it getting too dry. Meanwhile, heat the remaining butter in a separate pan, add the pancetta and sausage and fry until cooked through.

When the beef is ready, leave it to cool, then put it through a mincer with the pancetta and sausage. Put the minced meat in a bowl and combine with the Parmesan, egg and grated nutmeg to taste. Season with salt and pepper if necessary and set aside

Cut the pasta dough in half and flatten it slightly with a rolling pin. Pass each piece through a pasta machine on the widest setting, then fold in half and repeat, each time switching the machine to a finer setting, until the pasta is about 0.5mm thick. With a 6cm/2$\frac{1}{2}$in pastry cutter, cut a circle from the pasta and, using your fingers, stretch it as thinly as possible. Brush the edges with a little beaten egg and place a little of the filling in the middle, then fold the pasta over and draw back the edges to make a flower shape. Repeat until all the pasta and filling have been used. Keep the pasta dough covered with a damp cloth while you are working, to stop it drying out.

Bring the chicken stock to the boil in a large pan and drop in the *agnolini*. Simmer for about 4 minutes, until tender, then ladle into bowls and serve.

Basics

Always have plenty of good, full-flavoured stocks on hand – that is the true definition of social security. **Giorgio**

Giorgio's fish stock

Makes around 1 litre/1³/₄ pints

500g/1lb 2oz fish bones and heads
3 tablespoons olive oil
1 large onion, roughly chopped
1 leek, roughly chopped
1 celery stalk, roughly chopped

100ml/3¹/₂floz white wine
2 bay leaves
2 peppercorns
small bunch of flat-leaf parsley

Roughly chop the bones and soak them with the fish heads in plenty of cold water for 2 hours. Drain well.

Heat the oil in a large saucepan, add the bones and heads and cook gently for about 5 minutes. Add the chopped vegetables and cook for 2 minutes. Pour over the wine and then add around 1 litre/1³/₄ pints of cold water, or enough to cover the bones. Add the bay leaves, peppercorns and parsley and bring to the boil. Simmer for 20 minutes.

Using a ladle, pour the vegetables and fish through a fine sieve to extract all the juices. Bring the stock to the boil again and with a ladle skim off the residue that rises to the surface. Leave to cool, then store in the fridge or freezer.

Giorgio's chicken stock

Makes around 1 litre/1³/₄ pints

1kg/2¹/₄lb raw chicken carcasses
1 large onion, halved
2 carrots, quartered
2 celery stalks, halved

1 tablespoon tomato purée
1 bay leaf
8 black peppercorns
2 cloves

Preheat the oven to 190°C/375°F/Gas Mark 5. Put the chicken carcasses in a roasting tin and roast for 30 minutes. Add the onion, carrots and celery and continue to roast for 30 minutes. Spread the tomato purée over the carcasses and return to the oven for 3 minutes. Transfer the bones and vegetables to a stockpot or large saucepan and add the bay leaf, peppercorns and cloves. Cover with cold water and bring to the boil. Reduce the heat and simmer gently for 4 hours, skimming away any impurities that rise to the surface. Strain the stock through a fine sieve, pressing the vegetables with the back of a ladle to extract all the juices. Leave to cool, then store in the fridge or freezer.

Tony's vegetable stock

Makes about 1$\frac{1}{2}$ litres/2$\frac{1}{2}$ pints

2 tablespoons olive oil
2 onions, chopped
1 large carrot, chopped
2 celery stalks, chopped
1 leek, chopped
2 tomatoes, chopped (optional)

150g/5oz flat-cap mushrooms,
    chopped (optional)
2 garlic cloves, peeled but left whole
bunch of parsley stalks
2 sprigs of thyme
1 bay leaf

Heat the olive oil in a large pan, add the onions and cook over a medium heat until golden. Add the remaining vegetables and the herbs and cook gently for about 10 minutes, until softened. Pour in 1$\frac{1}{2}$ litres/2$\frac{1}{2}$ pints of water, bring to the boil and simmer for 45 minutes. Strain through a fine sieve and leave to cool. Store in a fridge or freezer.

Tony's beef stock

Makes about 1$\frac{1}{4}$ litres/2 pints

1.5kg/3lb beef bones (ask your
    butcher to chop them)
2 tablespoons olive oil
2 onions, roughly chopped
2 carrots, roughly chopped

2 celery stalks, roughly chopped
a few parsley stalks
1 bay leaf
5 black peppercorns

Preheat the oven to 220°C/425°F/Gas Mark 7. Put the bones in a roasting tin and place in the oven for about 1 hour, until browned.

Heat the olive oil in a large stockpot, add the vegetables and cook gently until softened but not coloured. Add the beef bones, parsley stalks, bay leaf and peppercorns and then pour in enough cold water to cover everything generously. Bring slowly to the boil, skimming off the scum as it rises to the surface. Simmer gently for about 4 hours, topping up with more water if necessary. Strain the stock through a fine sieve and leave to cool. Store in the fridge or freezer.

Tony's game stock

Makes about 1¼ litres/2 pints

1kg/2¼lb raw game carcasses
    (such as pigeon, pheasant etc)
1 tablespoon olive oil
1 onion, roughly chopped
1 carrot, chopped

1 celery stalk, chopped
1 bay leaf
2 sprigs of thyme
5 black peppercorns

Preheat the oven to 190°C/375°F/Gas Mark 5. Put the game carcasses in a roasting tin and roast for about 40 minutes, until browned.

    Heat the olive oil in a stockpot or large saucepan, add the vegetables and cook gently for about 10 minutes, until softened. Add the game carcasses to the pan with the bay leaf, thyme and peppercorns and cover with plenty of cold water. Bring slowly to the boil, skim off the scum from the surface, then reduce the heat and simmer very gently for about 3 hours, topping up with more water if necessary. Strain the stock through a fine sieve and leave to cool. Store in the fridge or freezer.

Giorgio's vinaigrette

Makes about 300ml/½ pint

½ teaspoon salt
50ml/2fl oz red wine vinegar

300ml/½ pint extra virgin olive oil
25ml/1fl oz water

Place the salt in a bowl, add the vinegar and leave to dissolve for a minute. Whisk in the olive oil and water until the vinaigrette emulsifies and thickens.

Giorgio's pasta dough

500g/1lb 2oz Italian 'OO' flour
pinch of salt

4 eggs

Sift the flour and salt into a food processor and, with the machine running, slowly pour in the eggs through the feed tube. As soon as the mixture comes together into a dough, switch off the machine. Put the dough on a lightly floured work surface and knead for 10–15 minutes, until smooth and elastic. Wrap in clingfilm and chill for 1 hour or so before use – if you don't allow it to rest, the dough will be quite difficult to roll and more likely to tear.

Tony's mayonnaise

Makes 300ml/½ pint

2 egg yolks
1 teaspoon Dijon mustard
2 tablespoons white wine vinegar

300ml/½ pint olive oil
salt and white pepper

Make sure all the ingredients are at room temperature. In a small bowl, beat the egg yolks with a little salt and white pepper, the mustard and half the vinegar. Add the oil a drop at a time, whisking constantly to give a thick, glossy emulsion; you can start to add the oil in a thin stream once about a third of it has been incorporated. Stir in the remaining vinegar and more seasoning to taste.

Tony's custard

Makes 300ml/ $\frac{1}{2}$ pint

300ml/ $\frac{1}{2}$ pint milk
1 vanilla pod

3 egg yolks, beaten
1 tablespoon caster sugar

Bring the milk and seeds from the split vanilla pod to the boil in a heavy-based saucepan. Meanwhile, whisk the egg yolks and sugar together in a bowl. Gradually whisk in the milk, then return the mixture to the rinsed-out saucepan. Stir over a gentle heat until the custard has thickened enough to coat the back of the spoon. Do not let it boil or it might curdle.

Tony's shortcrust pastry

175g/6oz plain flour
pinch of salt
75g/3oz unsalted butter, cut into
cubes

1 egg yolk
about 1 tablespoon iced water

Sift the flour and salt into a bowl, then rub in the butter with your fingertips until the mixture resembles fine crumbs. Make a well in the centre, add the egg yolk and water and mix together into a dough. If necessary, add a little more water, but be careful not to let the pastry become too wet. Knead very lightly for 30 seconds, until smooth, then wrap in clingfilm and chill for about 30 minutes before use.

Index

Acknowledgements

Tony

Thanks to my number-one kitchen brigade, my wife, Denys, and my beautiful daughters, Charlee and Hollie.

I'd also like to thank all the other kitchen brigades and staff at fish! and Bank restaurants around the country, especially the hugely talented Christian Delteil, with whom many of these recipes were conceived.

For making this book work I'd like to thank the amazing Giorgio, Louise Haines, Terry Durack, Kate Balmforth, Caz Hildebrand, Jason Lowe, Jane Middleton, Angela Boggiano and Jennifer White.

For making my life work, I'd like to thank Borra Garson, my mum and dad, sister-Nicky and Vinnie, Tanya and Kaylee Jones.

For service above and beyond the call of duty, a special thank you to the wonderful Sarah-Jane Rumble.

Giorgio

A very big thank you to my wife, Plaxy, and my kids, Margherita and Jack, for being the best taste testers and the most enthusiastic support team in the world. Thanks, too, to Borra Garson for her advice, help and friendship; to Louise Haines and Kate Balmforth of Fourth Estate, Terry Durack, and editor Jane Middleton, for their hard work and tireless belief in the project; and to Angela Boggiano and Jennifer White for testing our recipes with such care and intelligence.

Art director Caz Hildebrand and photographer Jason Lowe deserve special mention for making Tony and me look a lot better than we really do, while my entire team at Locanda Locatelli – especially the very talented Federico Sali – have proved once again that I am nothing without them.

I should also like to acknowledge the influence of two of the great Italian chefs in this country – Franco Taruschio, who established the Walnut Tree Inn in Wales, and Vincenzo Borgonzolo of London's Al San Vincenzo (that's him on page 26). With their wives, these two men showed us the true value of the family-run Italian restaurant, and set a fine example for Plaxy and me to follow.

Lastly, thanks to Tony Allan for being so much fun to work with.